Alphabetics for Emerging Learners

Discover how to help PreK students develop pre-reading competencies that build capacity for future reading—phonological awareness, print concepts, and alphabetics. Research-based and accessible, this essential guidebook helps educators sidestep common errors and to create an engaging, child-appropriate curriculum that lays a strong foundation for future reading skills. Filled with effective resources, activities, and a simple scope and sequence to guide instruction, this critical toolkit equips educators to set emerging learners up for success.

Heidi Anne E. Mesmer is Professor of Literacy in the School of Education at Virginia Tech, USA. A former classroom teacher, she works extensively with teachers, schools, and young readers, directing school-based initiatives to improve reading instruction.

Other Eye On Education Books

Available From Routledge
(www.routledge.com/k-12)

**Early Literacy Matters:
A Leader's Guide to Systematic Change**
Carol E. Canady, Robert Lynn Canady

**Coding as a Playground:
Programming and Computational Thinking in the Early Childhood Classroom**
Marina Umaschi Bers

**Implementing Project Based Learning in Early Childhood:
Overcoming Misconceptions and Reaching Success**
Sara Lev, Amanda Clark, and Erin Starkey

**Advocacy for Early Childhood Educators:
Speaking Up for Your Students, Your Colleagues, and Yourself**
Colleen Schmit

**Grit, Resilience, and Motivation in Early Childhood:
Practical Takeaways for Teachers**
Lisa B. Fiore

Alphabetics for Emerging Learners

Building Strong Reading Foundations in PreK

Heidi Anne E. Mesmer with Anna E. Kambach

NEW YORK AND LONDON

First published 2022
by Routledge
605 Third Avenue, New York, NY 10158

and by Routledge
2 Park Square, Milton Park, Abingdon, Oxon OX14 4RN

Routledge is an imprint of the Taylor & Francis Group, an informa business

© 2022 Heidi Anne E. Mesmer

The right of Heidi Anne E. Mesmer to be identified as author of this work has been asserted by them in accordance with sections 77 and 78 of the Copyright, Designs and Patents Act 1988.

All rights reserved. No part of this book may be reprinted or reproduced or utilised in any form or by any electronic, mechanical, or other means, now known or hereafter invented, including photocopying and recording, or in any information storage or retrieval system, without permission in writing from the publishers.

Trademark notice: Product or corporate names may be trademarks or registered trademarks, and are used only for identification and explanation without intent to infringe.

Library of Congress Cataloging-in-Publication Data
A catalog record for this title has been requested

ISBN: 978-0-367-67340-6 (hbk)
ISBN: 978-0-367-65168-8 (pbk)
ISBN: 978-1-003-13091-8 (ebk)

DOI: 10.4324/9781003130918

Typeset in Palatino
by Newgen Publishing UK

Dedication

For Beatrix Grace Allen, Elliott Reese Edelblute, and John Owen Edelblute IV, the three beautiful, curious emerging learners in my life.
~ Heidi Anne Mesmer

For my mother, Susan, who inspired a love of literacy, and for Matthew, Cecilia, and Elizabeth for whom I hope to do the same.
~ Anna Kambach

Contents

Meet the Authors   x

1 Beginning with Some Basics   1
This Book's Focus   3
   What is Alphabetics?   8
   What is Emergent Literacy?   8
Three Forced Choices You Do Not Have to Make   10
   Social Skills vs. Literacy Learning   11
   Play vs. Literacy Learning   12
   Meaningful Application vs. Focused Analysis of Letters   13
Literacy Development   14
Chapter Overviews   16

2 English Alphabetics for Teachers   20
What Is Writing and How Is It Different From Spoken Language?   22
A Brief (VERY brief) History of Writing   22
Alphabet: The Basis of English Writing   25
The Alphabetic Principle: How Do We Know When Young
   Children Have It?   26
The 44 English Phonemes   27
Major Letter-Sounds (GPCs) Taught in Early Years   29
Summary   33

3 Teaching Phonological Awareness   34
Basics   35
   Phonological Awareness is Not Phonics   35
   Phonemic Awareness Front Loads Letter-Sound Instruction
      Particularly for At-Risk Students   37
Best Practices in Phonological Awareness Instruction   37
Sounds: Larger Units, "Stretchable" Sounds, and Fewer
   Sounds are Easiest   38
   Size of Sound Units   39
   Types of Sounds (Easy to Stretch vs. Hard to Stretch)   40
   Number of Sounds   40
   Cues and Tasks: What Children Do with Sounds
      Influences Lesson Difficulty   41

	Oral, Physical, and Visual Cues	41
	Tasks: Receptive versus Expressive, Oddity, Isolation, and Segmenting	42
	Scope and Sequence for Daily Phonological Awareness	44
	Assessments for Phonological Awareness	52
	Activities and Games for Phonological Awareness	54
	Hand Motions	54
	Rhyming	55
	Words	56
	Syllables	57
	Initial Sounds	58
	Segmenting/Blending	58
	Chapter Summary	59
4	**Shared Reading and Interactive Writing to Teach Print Concepts and the Alphabetic Principle**	**62**
	What are "Concepts of Print?"	63
	Concept of Word: The Most Critical Print Concept	63
	Full Concept of Word	64
	No Concept of Word/Little Pointing	65
	Some Concept of Word	65
	Concept of Word Is NOT "Teaching Preschoolers to Read"	66
	Assessing Concepts of Print and Concept of Word	66
	A Simple Assessment for Concepts of Print	66
	Concept of Word in Print	66
	Shared Reading for Learning Print Concepts	66
	What is a "Shared Reading?"	69
	How to Do a Shared Reading	70
	Follow a Routine	71
	Shared Interactive Writing	76
	What is Shared Interactive Writing?	76
	How to Do an Interactive Writing Lesson	78
	A Few Cautions	81
	Other Techniques for Building Concepts of Print	82
	Finding Environmental Print EVERYWHERE	82
	Building a Play Environment to Enhance Literacy Exploration	82
	Fingerpoint "Reading" In Caption Books	83
	Chapter Summary	83
5	**Teaching Letters and Letter-Sounds**	**87**
	What Does it Mean to "Know Letters?" The Alphabetic Principle and Beyond	88

Naming letters	89
Letter-sounds	89
Writing letter forms	90
Using letters: The alphabetic principle	90
What You Should Know Before Teaching Letters	91
Visually Discriminating and Naming Letters is Only a First Step	92
The Typical Sequence in Which Children Learn Letters	93
Phonemic Awareness is the Key to Making Letter-Sounds "Stick"	94
Best Practices in Alphabet Instruction for Preschoolers	94
Be Systematic and Explicit	95
Teach Letters in Isolation but Model Use in Shared Reading and Writing	96
No More "Letter of the Week"	96
Choose Letters Purposefully	97
Cycle Through More Than One Letter Per Week and Review	99
Teach Short, Brisk, Predictable Lessons in Small Groups	99
Use Multisensory Techniques	100
Clip your Sounds on Stops: Avoid "Guh, Puh, Duh, Buh."	101
Assessment for Alphabet Instruction	101
What's the Goal in Preschool? How Many Letter-Names and Letter-Sounds?	101
Assess Names First, Then Sounds	103
Scope and Sequence for Alphabet Instruction	103
Activities for Alphabet Instruction	103
Awareness and Some Names: Exposure and Introduction	110
Environmental Print in My Community	111
Visual Discrimination and Naming	112
Advanced Letter Learning: Closing in on Letter-Sounds Writing Letters	113
Applying Letter Knowledge: The Essential Shared Reading and Writing Connection	113
Great Alphabet Books for Teaching Letter-Sounds	114
Summary	115
Appendix A	119
Appendix B	124
Appendix C	130
Appendix D	139

Meet the Authors

Heidi Anne E. Mesmer, PhD, is a Professor in Literacy at Virginia Tech. A former teacher, she has held tenure-earning positions for over 20 years. Dr. Mesmer has studied phonics, beginning reading materials, and text difficulty for her entire career. Her research has appeared in high impact journals including *Reading Research Quarterly, The Educational Researcher, Elementary School Journal,* and *Early Childhood Research Quarterly.* She has written and directed eight grants aimed at improving reading instruction in K-5 classrooms. She is the author of four books, including *Letter Lessons and First Words: Phonics Foundations that Work.*

Anna E. Kambach is a licensed teacher (Virginia PreK-6) who spent the first eight years of her teaching career teaching grades 1–3. She taught in an inclusive classroom, working with a wide range of learners including struggling readers, English Language Learners, and students in the gifted program. She received a Master's in Curriculum and Teaching from Teachers College, Columbia University and is currently a PhD student at Virginia Tech, focusing on emergent literacy.

1

Beginning with Some Basics

"You don't have to be great to start but you have to start to be great."
~ Zig Ziglar

We love this quote. It reminds us that starting is the key to doing anything well and sometimes starting is the hardest part—picking up pen and putting it to paper or cracking open the pages of a new book. So, thank you for choosing this book and for an interest in being a great early childhood educator. We take your investment of time seriously, and we promise to deliver high quality content to help you teach young children the foundations upon which later reading success are based.

So how did we come to write this book? Why did *we* start? Perhaps a little vignette from author Heidi Anne will set the stage. It tells about her experience in a classroom of three-year-olds.

> I will never forget an experience I had as I was conducting an early learning study in a three-year-old room. As I came into the classroom, I remember one of the teachers inviting me to come see the children. "We go over letters 30 minutes every day and they really know their letters," she said, possibly trying to impress me. I admit to having questions about spending that much time on letters in a three-year-old room, but one Friday, near the end of the study, I finally acquiesced, doubtful but agreeable. As I watched, I actually started to be impressed.

"Tt /tttt urtle/ Bb /bbbbbat/," the children said, as the teacher pointed to different letters on a chart.

I even noticed when the teacher took the pictures away and pointed to the letters, the children could identify those with the right beginning sound (apple, bat, etc.).

"These kids really do know their letters! They even know some sounds," I thought.

As I made my way around the room, I leaned in to talk to Jasmine, an adorable little girl with braids all over her head and bright pink barrettes. She was at a writing center using a marker and paper, making her best attempts to write the shapes of letters. Given what I had seen, I thought it would be fun to help her "spell" her name using the first letter. So, I started by pointing to an alphabet chart nearby and asking, "Which one is the letter Jj?" She immediately pointed to the Jj. "Wow! Now what sound for Jj?" Again, she said, "Jj is for jam," using the picture on the chart. "Wow," I thought, "this is pretty impressive for three-year-olds," as I dove into the next step, which revealed something very interesting.

"Let's write your name, Jasmin. Listen jjjjjjasmine. What letter should I use to start Jasmin?"

She looked up at me with a blank stare, and I looked back a little puzzled as well. I realized that she really did not understand how to use the letter-sound information that she had memorized. In fact, she was not able to apply it to a very important word—her name! She had not made the connection between the sound /j/ in *jam* and the /j/ in Jasmine. She was able to name the letter and was *saying* the right things, but she did not really *hear* the sound or connect the information. All that "alphabet" instruction was for naught. She could not use that information. What Jasmin had done was memorize information without knowing how to use it.

At some level, this might have been the seed for this book. The instructional approach here was not bad, but it would be best for children at least a year older. In addition, as Jasmin showed, letter instruction should never take place in a vacuum but should occur alongside meaningful practices that demonstrate the uses of letter knowledge.

This experience made us both realize that something is getting lost in translation. Between the standards, curricula, and professional developments on teaching the alphabet and the classroom practice, something is going wrong. Clearly, a straightforward resource focused specifically on how to teach letters and the related supports was needed. Clearly, something *for preschool* settings was needed. And so, this book was born.

As authors, we form a team with complimentary experiences and perspectives. Heidi Anne is a senior faculty member and literacy researcher who has been writing books for teachers and conducting literacy research for over 20 years. Anna is a new literacy researcher, living with her own set of preschoolers as a parent. Both of us are experienced teachers who have spent, and continue to spend, a great deal of time in classrooms with teachers and children. We have designed this book with care and a fair amount of honest feedback to create a pragmatic, research-based resource that can be opened up and used on a daily basis in the classroom.

This first chapter has several purposes. In the first section, we describe the book's focus—teaching alphabetics—and we say more about what we mean by *emergent* and *alphabetics*. We also show how our book connects to the Head Start Early Learning Outcomes domains. In the next section, we face a few controversies in the early childhood community and resolve them by noting that forced choices are not needed. Teachers do not need to choose between play and academics, or social–emotional learning and literacy, for example. In the third section, we layout typical literacy development, a path that educators must understand. In the last section, we provide an overview of the chapters in the book that take the reader from understanding how the English alphabet works to how to teach and assess what young children need to know in the areas of print concepts, phonological awareness, and letters.

This Book's Focus

Twenty years ago, a book entitled *Alphabetics for Emerging Learners* would have been improbable, but today's early childhood educator most certainly knows that teaching children the alphabet, phonological awareness, and print concepts are essential. At the onset, we want to be clear about two words that we use in this title, very purposefully—alphabetics and emerging. We also want to connect the book to current standards. Each state has its own preschool learning standards related to literacy, and many are similar. In order to ground this book with a common perspective, we refer to Head Start's Early Learning Outcomes Domains. There are three central domains, social/emotional, language and literacy, and cognition. This book focuses in the Language and Literacy central domain, which has two sections, Language and Communication, and Literacy. As the title suggests, the book will focus on the Literacy domain for children aged 36–60 months and, in particular, three out of the four subdomains, a) Phonological Awareness (P-Lit1); b) Print and Alphabet Knowledge—Print Concepts (P-Lit2); c) Print and Alphabet Knowledge—Alphabet Knowledge (P-Lit 3); and d) Writing (P-Lit 4, Spelling & Handwriting). For your convenience, these domains are specified across each of the two age ranges (i.e., 36–48 months, 48–60 months) in Table 1.1, below.

We can imagine that early childhood educators might be wondering, "But wait, isn't language and communication important too? What about the Comprehension subdomain of literacy (P-Lit 5)?" From our perspective, this book must dedicate precious space to thoroughly communicating all the solid research and best practices that support children's learning of letters, print concepts, and phonemes, vital information that is pivotal to their ability to decode and read words in the future. After several attempts to "squeeze it all

Table 1.1 Head Start's Early Learning Outcomes Domains: Three literacy domains focused on in this book

Developmental Progression		Indicators
36 to 48 Months	48 to 60 Months	By 60 Months
• Goal P-LIT 1. Child demonstrates an awareness that spoken language is composed of smaller segments of sound (Phonological Awareness)		
Shows rote imitation and enjoyment of rhyme and alliteration. With support, distinguishes when two words rhyme and when two words begin with the same sound.	Demonstrates rhyme recognition, such as identifying which words rhyme from a group of three: hat, cat, log. Recognizes phonemic changes in words, such as noticing the problem with "Old McDonald had a charm." Is able to count syllables and understand sounds in spoken words.	• Provides one or more words that rhyme with a single given target, such as "What rhymes with log?" • Produces the beginning sound in a spoken word, such as "Dog begins with /d/." • Provides a word that fits with a group of words sharing an initial sound, with adult support, such as "Sock, Sara, and song all start with the /s/ sound. What else starts with the /s/ sound?"

Table 1.1 Cont.

Developmental Progression		Indicators
• Goal P-LIT 2. Child demonstrates an understanding of how print is used (Functions of Print) and the rules that govern how print works (Conventions of Print)		
Distinguishes print from pictures and shows an understanding that print is something meaningful, such as asking an adult "What does this say?" or "Read this."	Begins to demonstrate an understanding of the connection between speech and print. Shows a growing awareness that print is a system that has rules and conventions, such as holding a book correctly or following a book left to right.	• Understands that print is organized differently for different purposes, such as a note, list, or storybook. • Understands that written words are made up of a group of individual letters. • Begins to point to single-syllable words while reading simple, memorized texts. • Identifies book parts and features, such as the front, back, title, and author.
• Goal P-LIT 3. Child identifies letters of the alphabet and produces correct sounds associated with letters		
Shows an awareness of alphabet letters, such as singing the ABC song, recognizing letters from one's name, or naming some letters that are encountered often.	Recognizes and names at least half of the letters in the alphabet, including letters in own name (first name and last name), as well as letters encountered often in the environment. Produces the sound of many recognized letters.	• Names 18 uppercase and 15 lowercase letters. • Knows the sounds associated with several letters.

(continued)

Table 1.1 Cont.

Developmental Progression		Indicators
<td colspan="3">• Goal P-LIT 4. Child demonstrates an understanding of narrative structure through storytelling/re-telling</td>
With support, may be able to tell one or two key events from a story or may act out a story with pictures or props.	Retells two or three key events from a well-known story, typically in the right temporal order and using some simple sequencing terms, such as first … and then.	• Re-tells or acts out a story that was read, putting events in the appropriate sequence, and demonstrating more sophisticated understanding of how events relate, such as cause and effect relationships. • Tells fictional or personal stories using a sequence of at least two or three connected events. • Identifies characters and main events in books and stories.
<td colspan="3">• Goal P-LIT 5. Child asks and answers questions about a book that was read aloud</td>
Child answers basic questions about likes or dislikes in a book or story. Asks and answers questions about main characters or events in a familiar story. With modeling and support, makes predictions about events that might happen next.	With support, provides basic answers to specific questions about details of a story, such as who, what, when, or where. With support, can answer inferential questions about stories, such as predictions or how/why something is happening in a particular moment.	• Answers questions about details of a story with increasingly specific information, such as when asked "Who was Mary?" responds "She was the girl who was riding the horse and then got hurt." • Answers increasingly complex inferential questions that require making predictions based on multiple pieces of information from the story, inferring characters' feelings or intentions, or providing evaluations of judgments that are grounded in the text.

Table 1.1 Cont.

Developmental Progression		Indicators
		• Provides a summary of a story, highlighting a number of the key ideas in the story and how they relate to each other.
• Goal P-LIT 6. Child writes for a variety of purposes using increasingly sophisticated marks (Spelling and Handwriting)		
Engages in writing activities that consist largely of drawing and scribbling. Begins to convey meaning. With modeling and support, writes some letter-like forms and letters.	Progressively uses drawing, scribbling, letter-like forms, and letters to intentionally convey meaning. With support, may use invented spelling consisting of salient or beginning sounds, such as L for elevator or B for bug.	• Creates a variety of written products that may or may not phonetically relate to intended messages. • Shows an interest in copying simple words posted in the classroom. • Attempts to independently write some words using invented spelling, such as K for kite. • Writes first name correctly or close to correctly. • Writes (draws, illustrates) for a variety of purposes and demonstrates evidence of many aspects of print conventions, such as creating a book that moves left to right.
Note: Publicly available document at: https://eclkc.ohs.acf.hhs.gov/interactive-head-start-early-learning-outcomes-framework-ages-birth-five		

in," we realized that high quality vocabulary and comprehension instruction in preschool is itself a meaty endeavor that should be thoroughly addressed in a book of this length. We did not want to relegate this content to a "check the box" chapter in a book about teaching alphabetics. (We would happily write such a book if invited.)

What is Alphabetics?

We think that when some readers see the word "alphabetics," they might think, "Is that a typo? Shouldn't it just say alphabet? Or is that word 'Alphabetics' just a fancy, new-fangled, ivory tower word that university people use?" We promise that we are not trying to show off when we use the term "alphabetics;" instead, we want to refer to a broader term, one that reflects better what preschool teachers of early literacy are actually doing. The word "alphabet" refers to the letters and the letter-sounds or grapheme-phoneme correspondences (GPCs). The word "alphabetics" refers to not only the letters and letter-sounds (GPCs) but also to the facets of literacy instruction that support learning letters. For example, phonemic awareness, the insight that words can be broken down into speech sounds (e.g., hat = /h/ /a/ /t/), undergirds or supports a child's ability to learn alphabet letters. Another example would be a child's understanding of how print works, that it runs left-to-right in English, that print carries the explicit message, that it runs from top to bottom. These insights are important if children are to apply their knowledge of alphabet letters. So, this book focuses not only on learning letters, but also on children acquiring all the understandings that support their use of alphabetic knowledge.

What is Emergent Literacy?

There is a term that we believe should be explained as we begin this book, "emergent literacy." First, what do we mean by "literacy?" In a recent blog, Heidi Anne writes, "One of the most pervasive misconceptions held by non-educators is that the words literacy and reading refer to the same thing." (For details, see this blog: 6 Myths of Kindergarten Literacy Instruction (Mesmer & Invernizzi, 2017). When we teach young children alphabetics and we also teach them comprehension and vocabulary through oral reading, we are engaging in *literacy* instruction. This broad term "literacy" refers not to "teaching young children to read," (i.e., "reading instruction") but, instead, to laying the foundation for eventual "reading" with broader literacy instruction.

Now, what do we mean by "emergent" and how is this different from "readiness?" (see Figure 1.1). Increasingly, we are hearing the term "readiness" floating around. We see things like "Reading Readiness" checklists. We hear about "readiness" assessments, like the Virginia Kindergarten Readiness Profile. Instead of "readiness," we prefer to use the term "emergent literacy," because it represents the nature of literacy learning better than the antiquated term "readiness." Let us explain with a little history lesson about "Reading Readiness."

Emergent Literacy	VS.	Reading Readiness
Literacy instruction is ongoing and continual		Reading instruction begins when a child is "ready"
Literacy instruction responds to emerging child knowledge		Reading instruction begins when a specific criterion is reached (e.g. age 6 years, 6 months)
Growing and changing		Static, point-in-time
Always "in" Always learning		In vs. out of instruction Ready vs. "not ready"
Focus on creating the conditions for reading–an ongoing process		Children must be made "ready" to read
Focuses broadly on the development of literacy including phonological awareness, oral language, letters, print concepts, vocabulary, and comprehension		Focuses specifically on learning to read and decode

Figure 1.1 Emergent Literacy vs. Reading Readiness.

From about 1900 to the mid-1960s, one of the main theories about beginning reading instruction was that of "readiness." People thought that a child's biological maturation or age should determine when he received formal literacy instruction and usually that was kindergarten or first grade (Gesell, 1925). In fact, two educators, Washburne and Morphett (1931), actually had a precise mental age (6 years, 6 months) when they believed reading instruction should begin. During this time, this highly influential theory resulted in literacy instruction of any sort being held off until the latter half of first grade.

In the 1960s and 1970s, researchers found that reading success had little to do with a child's age or readiness and more to do with exposure to and even direct literacy instruction (e.g., Clay, 1966; Durkin, 1966; Read, 1975; Schickedanz & Marchant, 2018; Teale & Sulzby, 1986). In her 1966 dissertation, Marie Clay coined the term "emergent literacy." Others supported this idea and explained that from birth, children are emerging as literate beings gradually acquiring the many competencies they will access once they begin formal reading instruction. Oral language development, vocabulary, expressive language, and listening comprehension all feed later literacy. Language play and an awareness of sounds and rhyme build capacity for the phoneme-based alphabet we use.

We embrace the idea of "emergent" literacy and view the term as more appropriate, especially with early childhood. No doubt, many people could be using the term "readiness" in non-specific ways. Sometimes they are actually capturing much of the information that we know to be appropriate to teaching young children. Nonetheless, "readiness" is simply not a term that we really like.

You have heard the teacher who says, "They are just not ready," often to mean "we are cramming inappropriate instruction down this kid's throat" (a point we agree with). However, using that "readiness" term introduces a dividing line between those who are and those who are not. For example, if a young child is not "ready," does that mean they are "unready?" Does that mean they need readiness instruction? Why not just assess them and teach what they do not know without the label? If a child is not "ready," does that mean someone failed to "prep" them? The "readiness" label tends to put the responsibility of being ready on the parent or child or last year's teacher—someone who is not immediately available. As professional educators, we believe every child is "ready" and emerging as a literate being. It's schools, teachers, or classrooms that are not ready—not ready with the right curriculum, the right lesson, or the right assessments. Truly, we should be talking about teacher readiness, classroom readiness, or school readiness as opposed to student readiness.

Three Forced Choices You Do Not Have to Make

Maybe you have met a teacher who says something like this, "We are pushing down too much academic stuff into preschool. I am not having any of it. We are just going to play, do puzzles, go outside, and listen to stories. Children learn through play." Conversely, perhaps you have heard some "expert" from your state or university drone on about the importance of alphabetic knowledge and phonemic awareness instruction in preschool. Unfortunately, people sometimes take extremes when it comes to the early childhood classroom. There are those who reject any type of teaching of the alphabet and then there are those who, like my friend in the three-year-old room, are offering instruction that is not hitting the mark.

We are here to tell you that it does not have to be that way! You do not have to choose between literacy and play, social emotional learning and academic learning, cognitive development and the whole child. You can do both! It is not a forced choice. In fact, good literacy instruction should be fun! It should engage, challenge, delight, and progress young children. Literacy is all around them, and they usually want to be part of the club! In fact, if your literacy instruction does not engage children, if they do not know what to do with what they are learning, or they do not have some keen interest in it, then you are doing it wrong.

The simple fact is that we cannot afford these extremes. As a slew of research shows us, emotional and psychological learning and healing are essential if young children are to thrive. Those little three-year-olds chiming the alphabet were more than brains. They were hearts and spirits, too. The opposite is true as well. Sometimes, in a push back to legitimately inappropriate expectations, assessments, or curricula, teachers throw the baby out with the bathwater. We cannot roll back decades of important work that shows us that young learners, often the most at-risk learners, benefit greatly from great literacy instruction in preschool.

Social Skills vs. Literacy Learning

Perhaps more than any other group in education, early childhood educators embrace the importance of children developing their social and emotional selves. They know that whatever they become in life, they will be humans, and must be supported in working with others and understanding themselves. Without these abilities, children will not learn anything academic.

In particular, children must learn "social skills" and "self-regulation." Social skills is a broad term that usually refers to the competencies a child has interacting with peers and adults. It can include, for example, making friends, getting along, not being oppositional, following directions, and keeping one's hands to oneself. In a very interesting study, researchers proved something that many early childhood educators know already—children who possess social skills are better able to learn (Spira, Bracken, & Fischel, 2005). These researchers examined children's social skills and literacy skills in kindergarten and found that those who had skills in both of these areas were doing the best by fourth grade. In other words, social skills make learning possible.

The same holds true for another, more specific, skill, self-regulation (Blair, 2002). This refers to a child's ability to control his/her emotions and respond appropriately (e.g., get in line for outdoor play when you really want to stay and finish the puzzle). It also means regulating your attention to complete tasks. Children who have age-normal self-regulation skills can participate in instruction, learn, complete tasks, and not be distracted. Self-regulation is different from intelligence or cognitive ability. Importantly, we know that a child's ability to self-regulate will influence their learning (see Figure 1.2). It makes sense that in order to learn and focus on songs, alphabet, rhymes, stories, numbers, or colors, children must be able to control impulses and

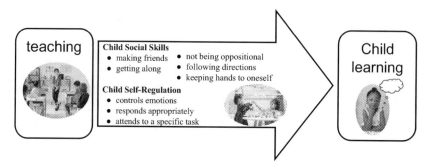

Figure 1.2 Social Skills and Self-Regulation Enable Learning.

move forward from distracting emotions. If we do not help young children self-regulate and acquire social skills, they will not learn. These skills mediate or enable learning and without them attention will not be given to the content to be learned.

Play vs. Literacy Learning

Early childhood educators know more than anyone the importance of play in learning. Not only is play enjoyable for children and good for the development of social skills, to young children play *is* learning. As we've said before, good literacy instruction should be fun! A child-centered program that integrates play improves literacy learning.

Research supports the connection between literacy learning and certain types of play. Specifically, the ability to engage in symbolic play can actually improve a child's understanding of what reading is (Stone & Stone, 2007). Symbolic play is when children begin to use an object to represent something that it's not (e.g., using a block as a telephone). For example, after being introduced to The Magic School Bus, Anna's son began using his white board as an iPad to do "research" as he played out scenes similar to those in the books.

Children engaging in symbolic play are often seen as imaginative or creative but it's more than that. Symbolic play is a vertical cognitive advance that translates into other areas of the child's life. One research summary found that symbolic play "improves decontextualized language and narrative skills that support later comprehension" (Pellegrini, 1985). Decontextualized language is when we talk about something that is not physically present in the here and now. It's like listening to a story that has already happened. In the same way that symbolic play requires a child to represent one object using another, reading requires the insight that a word "object" represents the real thing (Stone & Stone, 2007). For example, children who know that the word "snow" refers to the real frozen, white precipitation, are accessing symbolic understandings. When a teacher reads a story about snow and it's not snowing outside, they are showing an understanding of decontextualized language. They are showing that they understand that written words represent something in our speech and in our environment.

Teachers can use this information in the classroom when planning how to include play in literacy instruction. You get to design this play intentionally based on your knowledge of literacy and, most importantly, your students. Specific ways that educators can use play to promote literacy was described by Neuman and Roskos (1990) and Morrow and Rand (1991). They found value in teaching literacy through play. Teaching alphabetic knowledge and phonemic awareness are not enough on their own; early childhood educators must provide "highly engaging interactions that honor the child's intrinsic motivations to learn within his or her environment" (Mesmer & Rose-McCully, 2018). You don't have to choose between teaching literacy skills and letting students play. Early childhood educators make the content both enjoyable and relevant to kids. You get the great opportunity to create authentic learning opportunities for your students, which can be done through play.

Meaningful Application vs. Focused Analysis of Letters

This is the last forced choice that we see teachers believing they must make. It usually sounds something like this: "Reading is all about meaning, and we should *only* teach letters within the context of meaningful experiences like using labeling, reading books, or writing messages," versus "The way to teach letters is one-by-one by individually analyzing each one. *After they learn letters*, children can be taught how to apply it all in reading and writing." With the exception of the italicized words, both of these statements are true. First, in order to learn over 26 letter symbols (some uppercase and lowercase letters do not look the same) and related sounds, children will need to work with each individually, in isolation. This is how they really study a letter and see how it differs from others. This is how they practice learning the letter-sound correspondences or grapheme-phoneme correspondences (GPCS). Without focused analysis of isolated letters, learning will not occur. However, we cannot wait until after children "learn their letters" to show them how to use that knowledge. The example with Jasmine makes this abundantly clear. Without an understanding of the "big picture," we are wasting our time. Little children will memorize to please *us*, but it will not help them. Throughout this book, and in Chapter 4 in particular, we will make the case that shared reading and interactive writing must take place several times a week alongside letter instruction. These practices model how reading and writing work, and, with patience, they pay off.

Literacy Development

We want to give you a brief overview of literacy development before we really get started. Reading involves two categories of skills: word recognition and language comprehension. Word recognition means skills such as decoding (being able to use letter-sound knowledge to sound out written words), sight recognition (words that do not require decoding), and phonological awareness. Language comprehension includes background knowledge, vocabulary, understanding how language is structured, verbal reasoning, and literacy knowledge (Scarborough, 2001). That's a lot to say that students need to be able to both read the words and understand the words in order to be a fluent reader. You can think of this like the equation $1 \times 1 = 1$. This statement is true, but if you change one of the factors to zero, the product becomes zero. Now, let's make the equation *word recognition x language comprehension = reading*. Similarly, if you change one of the factors to zero, such as if you have a student who doesn't have word recognition, then the product (reading) becomes a zero as well. A child cannot be a strong reader without developing both pieces. We must also say that although The Simple View of Reading (Gough & Tunmer, 1986) is supported by research (e.g., Hoover & Gough, 1990; Catts, Adlof, & Weismer, 2006), it is a basic framework that has been criticized for its oversimplification of reading. We recognize this and want you to know that the makeup of a strong reader is much more complicated.

Before children can develop these reading skills, there are skills that have to come first; this work begins long before kindergarten. Starting at birth, children are exposed to language and literacy. You know that all children do not have the same exposure, but that early experiences shape our future. We will briefly explain some of the key skills developed prior to reading to provide you with an overview and definition of the skills we will discuss later (see Figure 1.3). In order to learn to read, children must have an understanding of:

- concepts of print
- letter-sound correspondence
- phonological awareness
- vocabulary
- background knowledge

As an early childhood educator, you play a key role in this early development of underlying skills. You set the stage for this work to be done in kindergarten

Beginning with Some Basics ◆ 15

Term	Definition	Example
concept of print	A variety of skills having to do with how books and printed text function.	1. Holding a book correctly 2. Looking at the pages from front-to-back of the book and from left to right on the pages 3. Start reading at the top of the page. 4. Knowing a letter versus a word 5. Identify punctuation and its function 6. Know the difference between a capital and lowercase letter.
letter-sound correspondence	knowing how letters in the alphabet represent certain sounds in speech.	Knowing that the b in "bear" makes the /b/ sound.
phonological awareness	ability to identify and use parts of speech such as words, syllables, onset (initial sound heard) and rimes (vowel and consonants that follow).	1. Creating rhymes, such as cat-hat-sat. 2. Identifying that sat, silly, and song all begin with the /s/ sound.
vocabulary	understanding of word meanings	When reading, *Those Darn Squirrels* by Adam Rubin, new words such as "overjoyed" need to be explained so children can understand the character feeling that emotion, in this case it's the squirrels.
background knowledge	Information based on previous experiences	When reading *Corduroy* for the first time, Anna had to explain to her son what an escalator is and why Corduroy might call it a mountain. He knew from his prior experience that this was clearly not a mountain, but living in a small town, he had no experience with escalators and didn't know their function.

Figure 1.3 Literacy Terms to Know.

and beyond. The work you do is enabling this work to be done. Through your joyful, fun, engaging curriculum, you lay the literacy foundation for your students.

Chapter Overviews

So, what do we have in store in this book? We have worked out the essentials of teaching alphabetics in the remaining chapters in the book. These chapters are packed with information and graphics that will allow you to immediately assess and teach preschoolers print concepts, alphabet, and phonological awareness. We provide a sneak peek of the chapters here so that you can grab them when you need to or skip ahead if there is something that you need to know right now.

In Chapter 2, English Alphabetics for Teachers, we give you some basic background about the English writing system that will help you to understand what writing is, how we typically organize letter-sounds, and how the system works. English is an alphabetic system. Along with other alphabetic systems, it reflects one of the most amazing inventions of all time. At times it can be confusing, but it is a system. In this chapter we will tell the story of how written systems came into being, identify the 44 English phonemes, specify the major categories of letter-sounds that we teach children, and provide essential definitions for words like consonant, vowel, and phoneme.

In Chapters 3 to 5, we provide specific information for three components of literacy instruction in preschools—phonological awareness, print concepts, and letters (GPCs). Each of these chapters is rich with resources, graphics, and ready-to-go resources for your preschool classroom. Chapter 3, *Teaching Phonological Awareness*, provides support for the important oral insights that children must have about words, syllables, and individual sounds. When children are aware that oral words are composed of individual speech sounds, they are more likely to learn letter-sounds more easily. This chapter explains what phonological awareness is and how it develops. The chapter also includes a simple oral assessment that teachers can give to their students to understand what they know about sounds, and it includes a sequence of instruction from the easiest sound units to the most difficult. The last part of Chapter 3 includes lively activities and book suggestions for supporting phonological awareness instruction.

Chapter 4 focuses on the Print Conventions (Concepts of Print) domain or the insights that children gain about how print works (e.g., left-to-right, front/back of book, print carrying meaning). The chapter also explains the key print convention—understanding how words work in print. Included in this chapter is a very simple five-minute print concepts assessment and a separate "concept of word" assessment for more advanced preschoolers. The chapter highlights and provides step-by-step instructions for two practices that we believe should be daily events—shared reading and interactive writing. Both of these practices illustrate for young children how reading and writing work and both involve children in helping their teacher as she reads and writes.

Chapter 5, *Learning Letters*, provides everything you need to know about teaching letters. We start with some basic research about letters. Did you know that some letters are easier to learn than others? Some letter-names actually help children learn sounds. This chapter also includes an assessment, a scope and sequence, and a collection of activities. We really do have to get letters right in the preschool classroom, and this chapter helps.

Summary

In closing this chapter, we want to say a bit about research. Of course, this book is research-based. We have carefully examined the research and worked hard to translate it into useful practice. We have both been classroom teachers and know what it is like to have research pushed on you. This is not how we want research to be viewed. When we were in the classroom, we knew it was difficult to find time to use the restroom, respond to a parent, or wipe down a table, much less dig into new research and apply it to our instruction. As dedicated professionals like yourselves, we loved learning and understanding what was happening in the research world, but reading studies or articles just didn't always happen. Our time instead went to communicating with parents, planning engaging lessons, and attending faculty meetings.

As researchers, we get the opportunity to translate and share new findings and methods with teachers. We are able to take time to identify where large amounts of evidence support particular ways of doing things and share these with you. We enjoy being able to put information together and provide suggestions, but it is not our intention to force anything on you. You are with your students in classrooms every single day and know what it takes to make learning happen. We feel that researchers and educators have different, yet complementary, roles. The expertise that we bring to the table may be different, but both are equally as important in designing quality-reading instruction for students. Our hope is that educators and researchers can build a respectful, equitable relationship and work together to create the best learning opportunities for students.

As you dive into this book, we hope to empower you. What do you want your students to know at the end of their preschool year? As you are reading this book, we feel certain that you want your students to head off to kindergarten with some literacy knowledge. You probably also want your students to have other academic knowledge when they leave your care, such as how to count objects or use their senses to observe the world around them. Now, what do you think your students will remember most about their time in preschool with you? When asked, they probably won't respond with "my teacher taught us all the skills we needed to succeed in kindergarten." Instead, they will remember the art that you created, the time you spent gathered together reading aloud, or maybe riding tricycles. Even if you are thinking of something else they might remember, something unique to your classroom, you are probably thinking of something joyful. Academics and joyful experiences are not a one or the other situation. Early childhood educators know this more than anyone! We are glad you are here to get to know more about literacy instruction. Be assured that joy is a part of the process.

References

Blair, C. (2002). School readiness: Integrating cognition and emotion in a neurobiological conceptualization of children's functioning at school entry. *American Psychologist, 57*(2), 111.

Catts, H. W., Adlof, S. M., & Weismer, S. E. (2006). Language deficits in poor comprehenders: A case for the simple view of reading. *Journal of Speech, Language, and Hearing Research, 49,* 278–293.

Clay, M. M. (1966). *Emergent reading behaviour* (Doctoral dissertation, ResearchSpace@ Auckland).

Durkin, D. (1966). The achievement of pre-school readers: Two longitudinal studies. *Reading Research Quarterly, 1*(4), 5–36.

Gesell, A. (1925). *The mental growth of the pre-school child: A psychological outline of normal development from birth to the sixth year, including a system of developmental diagnosis.* New York: MacMillan

Gough, P. B., & Tunmer, W. E. (1986). Decoding, reading, and reading disability. *Remedial and Special Education, 7*(1), 6–10.

Hoover, W. A., & Gough, P. B. (1990). The simple view of reading. *Reading and Writing, 2*(2), 127–160.

Mesmer, H. A. (2017). *Six myths about kindergarten literacy instruction.* Heinemann Publishing. https://medium.com/@heinemann/6-myths-about-kindergarten-literacy-instruction-38c24b984eb0.

Mesmer, H. A., & Rose-McCully, M. M. (2018). A closer look at close reading: Three under-the-radar skills needed to comprehend sentences. *The Reading Teacher, 71*(4), 451–461.

Morrow, L. M., & Rand, M. K. (1991). Promoting literacy during play by designing early childhood classroom environments. *The Reading Teacher, 44*(6), 396–402.

Neuman, S., & Roskos, K. (1990). Play, print, and purpose: Enriching play environments for literacy development. *The Reading Teacher, 44*(3), 214–221. Retrieved December 15, 2020, from www.jstor.org/stable/20200594

Pellegrini, A. D. (1985). Relations between preschool children's symbolic play and literate behavior. *Play, Language and Stories: The Development of Children's Literate Behavior, 56*(1), 79–97.

Read, C. (1975). *Children's categorization of speech sounds in English* (No. 17). National Council of Teachers of English.

Scarborough, H. (2001). Connecting early language and literacy to later reading (dis)abilities: Evidence, theory and practice. In S. Newman & D. Dickinson (Eds.), *Handbook of early literacy research.* pp. 97–110. New York, Guilford Press.

Schickedanz, J. A., & Marchant, C. (2018). *Inside pre-k classrooms: A school leader's guide to effective instruction.* Harvard Education Press.

Spira, E. G., Bracken, S. S., & Fischel, J. E. (2005). Predicting improvement after first-grade reading difficulties: The effects of oral language, emergent literacy, and behavior skills. *Developmental Psychology, 41*(1), 225.

Stone, S. J., & Stone, W. (2007). Symbolic play and emergent literacy. In *Brno conference, International Council for Children's Play*, Eds. Brno, Chezhia: Brno Conference.

Teale, W. H., & Sulzby, E. (1986). *Emergent literacy: Writing and reading. Writing research: Multidisciplinary inquiries into the nature of writing series.* Ablex Publishing Corporation.

Washburne, C., & Morphett, M. W. (1931). When should elementary children begin to read? *Elementary School Journal, 31*(7), 496–503.

2

English Alphabetics for Teachers

What do you need to know about the letters and sounds and print before you begin teaching young children? It would seem not a lot. Just teach kids the letters and sounds and have them put it together to read. As it turns out, teachers need to know more than you may think! Just because you can read and write yourself does not mean that you have full command of how an alphabet, writing, and the English system works. In fact, well-known literacy educator Dr. Moats (2020) recently reprised a 1999 article entitled *Teaching Reading is Rocket Science, 2020: What expert teachers of reading should know and be able to do.* As the story below from Heidi Anne will attest, lessons can go awry without some basic understanding, and teachers who do not have some basics down can waste a lot of time. Here is a little peek into a less-than-optimal alphabet lesson. See if you can spot the mistakes.

> I will never forget my early letter lessons with young children. Although well intentioned, I often made mistakes because I did not fully understand the content I was teaching—the sounds, the letter representations. A disastrous lesson on the letters Ff and Vv went something like this:
>
> This is the letter Ff. It makes the sound /f/ like *foot, fish,* and *fun.* Can you hear that *fffffoot, fffffffish,* and *ffffun. /f/?* Can you say that sound /f/? Can you point to the letter on your alphabet strip?

DOI: 10.4324/9781003130918-2

We are also going to learn this letter [pointing to Vv]. Does anyone know this letter? Yes, Victor, it is Vv like in your name *Vvvvvvictor*. Vv makes the sound /v/. Like in *vase, van,* and *vegetable*.

Okay, now that we know these two sounds, let's play a game. I am going to show a picture and you tell me the sound. Here is a *vegetable*. Is it /f/ like *fish* or /v/ like *vase?*

If you are an experienced teacher, you can likely guess how this lesson continued. In a nutshell, when I asked children to name sounds for Ff and Vv they got mixed up. The children kept telling me the /v/ sound for Ff words and vice versa. And, like any frustrated teacher I just kept saying the same things over and over, "Wait, listen, does *vvvvvegetable* have the sound /f/ at the beginning? Isn't it /v/?"

I had chosen these two letters because they are visually distinct—the Ff and the Vv have very different shapes—but I had failed to recognize several things about these two sounds. First. any experienced speech-language specialist would be able to spot one issue—the sounds for the letters Ff and Vv are really quite similar in how they are made in the mouth. They are made in the same place in the mouth and in the same way, with the lips close together and a stream of air being pushed through. The only difference is that the sound for Vv is voiced (e.g., your voice box buzzes when you say that sound) and Ff is unvoiced (there is no buzzing). So, these sounds are really quite similar, and it was likely difficult for the children to hear or feel the differences. This was not a pair of letters that should have been taught adjacently. This pair was not a good set to contrast because the differences are slight. Another problem is that developmentally, many young children cannot make the sound for the letter Vv until about 48 months. So, even if a child could tell the difference between the sounds /f/ and /v/, many children would not be able to properly make the sound /v/.

What this little vignette illustrates is that teachers must have concrete knowledge about alphabets, writing, and sounds (Moats 2020; Wong Fillmore & Snow, 2000). If Heidi Anne had known just a little bit more about the content, so many issues could have been avoided. The six sections in this chapter reveal basic information about how writing works and how it developed historically and how phoneme-based alphabets represent a critical invention. Later sections underscore the importance of the alphabetic principle, name the 44 English phonemes, and then identify the major letter-sound categories taught in preschool and early childhood. There are several boxes and guides throughout, including one to help with alphabet strips and pictures used in them.

What Is Writing and How Is It Different From Spoken Language?

The alphabet is a new symbol system for young children, challenging them to think differently about words and to acquire strange insights. As adults, we often assume children have understandings that they do not, such as what the letters in an alphabet represent. But to start, we need to differentiate alphabets from other writing systems and explain how writing itself developed.

Speech and writing are different. Speech is an oral and aural (heard) system of sounds that communicates a message (e.g., the spoken message "I will go to the store."). Writing is "speech written down," a system of visual symbols that represents the transient oral/aural message. Writing "nails down" an oral message so that it can be preserved across time and space when the messenger and the receiver are not in the same physical place. Writing is the mirror image of speech. Writing translates a spoken message into a code of symbols that can be shared. However, writing is not actually a primary characteristic of language. It came along after spoken language—quite a bit after.

Have you ever heard this? "Becoming literate is as natural as speaking. Children become literate in the same way they learn to speak, by being surrounded with literacy, hearing stories, and playing with books." This is actually untrue. For almost all humans, spoken language is learned without explicit instruction while written language requires explicit instruction. Although the majority of children learn to speak by being spoken to, having their speech responded to, and by participating in a speech community, that is not the way most children become literate. Writing is an invention that seems to have appeared around the third millennium BC. The English alphabetic system that we use today, based on phonemes or speech sounds, is even newer. It followed simpler forms of writing. Alphabets are efficient and parsimonious but not intuitive and not the first attempt to encode speech.

A Brief (VERY brief) History of Writing

The earliest attempts to "write down" speech were actually pictographs, pictorial symbols that directly resembled the word or phrase being depicted (e.g., *goat, shoot arrow*). Literally, the term pictograph is from the Latin picto (painted) + graph (writing). Pictographs were the forerunners to writing. They are easily interpretable, and you need no special training to learn them. You look at the pictograph and it looks like what it is (See Table 2.1).

Over time, the pictographs in written systems became consistent and standardized, meaning that every time a particular group of people symbolized *goat* they would do so with the exact same patterns and marks. Increasingly the pictographs became extended to ideographs (idea writing) to represent a collection of ideas. For example, the pictograph for water, a drop of water, might represent several ideas—*rain, water,* or *thirst.* Although easy to learn, pictographs and ideographs are problematic because some words are abstract and cannot be pictured (e.g., *love*) and the system can lack precision.

Eventually, pictographs became more symbolic and logographic. A logograph is an agreed upon symbol for a word or morpheme that can depict items, ideas, verbs, and other rich, important words. The word logograph, in Latin, means logo (word) + graph (writing). Thus, logographs represented a clear step to symbolizing individual words. Logographs are different from pictographs in that they do not always look like the items being depicted. Logograph users agree on a meaning, as in the symbol ♥ representing love,

Table 2.1 Types of Written Systems

	Represents	Relationship to Sound	Word	Written Example
Pictograph	Word or phrase with a picture. Symbol looks like the word being depicted	Symbol does not represent sound.	deer	
Ideograph	Word, phrase, or idea with a picture. Symbol looks like the word(s) being depicted.		water, thirst, rain,	
Logograph	Word with an agreed-upon symbol. Symbol may or may not look like the word being depicted.		love	
Syllabary	A syllable with a symbol. Symbol does not look like word being depicted.	Symbol represents a syllable. Depict language sounds.	re	
Alphabet	A phoneme with a symbol. Symbol does not look like word being depicted.	Symbol represents a speech sound (c-a-t)	cat	C= /k/ A= /a/ T = /t/

but the symbol does not always look like the word being represented. A heart does not "look like" love.

There were problems with logographs, especially with the number of words being represented. Languages can contain up to 50,000 words and depicting even a small number of these words through individual logographs places a big burden on human memory. Memorizing thousands of symbols takes a lot of time. (This is why users of logographic writing systems like Chinese actually invented alphabetic formats such as Pinyin to teach young children how to read.) Humans have a hard time learning this many individual symbols and the learning burden became so great in the ancient world that only certain classes of people had the time to become literate.

The next step in the development of writing was to move away from symbolizing words to symbolizing the *sounds* in a language. Why? Because languages have far fewer *sounds* than they do *words*. The first sound-based writing used logographs to symbolize syllables. For example, one symbol would be used to depict the syllable *ren*. Cherokee writing represents syllables. Syllabic systems work for languages that are regular at the syllable level but not all languages are. As described in the next section, written systems eventually moved to using alphabetic symbols to represent individual speech sounds (e.g., r = /r/, e = /e/, n = /n/).

BOX 2.1 Writing Letters and Writing Sounds in This Book

Writing letters and writing sounds in this book

Writing about sounds in a book like this is tricky. How do you tell the reader when you are talking about a "sound," versus a "letter?" In this book, when we mean a letter, we will write both the upper and lowercase forms together (e.g., "Vv," "Tt"), as in, "The letter Bb is at the beginning of Bryce's name."

To represent sounds, linguists use a specific alphabet called the International Phonetic Alphabet, because it has a special symbol for each sound (see below). They must use special symbols like ə, ʃ, and θ, because we have more sounds in our language (~44) than letters (26). However, we find that teachers do not have a fluency with IPA symbols and so, when we are referring to a sound in this book, we will use slash marks (e.g., /ay/ = the sound in p-*ai*-n; /t/ = the sound in *t*-oy).

Alphabet: The Basis of English Writing

In the history of written systems, the next step was alphabetic. Alphabets use letters to represent an even smaller unit of sound than syllabaries, the phoneme or speech sound. A phoneme is the smallest unit of sound in a spoken language that differentiates the meaning of a word (e.g., *hat* versus *hit*). So, in these two words the phonemes /i/ and /a/ differentiate these words, so that one refers to a piece of clothing to wear on the head and the other refers to striking an object. The word *hit* has three letters and three phonemes /h /i/ /t/. There is a one-to-one relationship between the letters and the phonemes. Technically, we call the visual, written representation of a phoneme a grapheme. Thus, educators will use the term grapheme-phoneme correspondences (GPCs) to mean what has traditionally been called letter-sound correspondences. As described below, not all graphemes have only one letter. English has 44 sounds but only 26 letters, so, to represent some phonemes, it combines letters (e.g., *th, ch, oi, oy*). Thus, a grapheme in English can be made up of one *or more* letters.

Regular, orderly alphabets have a letter symbol for each phoneme in the language (e.g., Spanish). There is one letter symbol for each sound. We call these transparent orthographies because they are transparent, nothing complicated: they are straightforward.

The English alphabet is not so orderly. We have more sounds than letters. Some words do have a one-to-one relationship between letters and sounds (e.g., dog, bag) but for others we must combine letters to represent sounds (e.g., sh, ch, th, ee/ea/ey). It also means that letter order influences sounds. A Yy at the end of a word is more likely to represent a vowel sound (e.g., ba**y**, cr**y**) than a consonant sound (e.g., **y**ak, **y**et). A Cc followed by an Ee or Ii will usually represent the sound /s/ (e.g., *cent, city*). When a Cc is followed by an Aa, Oo, or Uu it will have the sound /k/ (e.g., *cab, cop, cup*). English also has a unique history. It was developed on an island that experienced multilingual invaders. English spellings respect word origins (e.g., in Greek-derived words, the "ch" represents the sound /k/ as in *chorus, Christian,* and *chiropractor*).

Some people incorrectly tell children, "English makes no sense, so just memorize it," but that is inaccurate. Although a deep alphabet, English *is* an alphabet, nonetheless, and should be taught as one. The complications, however, mean that teaching English phoneme-grapheme relationships require a more systematic approach, one that sequences instruction from the easiest patterns to the most complex. We typically teach one-to-one correspondences before two-to-one or three-to-one correspondences.

The Alphabetic Principle: How Do We Know When Young Children Have It?

The alphabetic principle is simply the understanding that letter symbols represent speech sounds. It is essential if children are to make any use of alphabet knowledge in any way. Janice, a veteran teacher, explains what letter instruction looks like without an understanding of the system: "Well, I was teaching them letters and sounds but they did not have a clue what that meant. I might as well have been teaching them widgets and doodads. They could tell me, 'This is Aa,' or that makes the sound '/a/,' but they didn't really 'get' the whole idea, the system. When I asked them about spelling words, or even thinking about using sounds to find words, they didn't have a clue."

As we learned from Jasmin in the first chapter, children *can* actually learn exactly what we *teach* them through imitation, but this does not mean that they can really use the information or understand the reason that they are learning it. In order to help children understand the alphabetic system, we must model and illustrate it through practices like shared reading and interactive writing. Using these techniques, described in Chapter 4, teachers show children how letter-sound (phoneme-grapheme) information is used during authentic reading and writing. These practices must parallel letter instruction and occur on a daily basis.

The interaction below shows preschoolers who are in different places in terms of understanding the alphabetic principle:

Teacher: "Okay, now I want to write the word *fire* in our sentence: *They put out the fire.* What sound is at the beginning of fffffire?"
James: "Crackle, crackle?"
Darion: "Fire!" (He says very loudly.)
Tessa: "/er/?"

Cute, aren't they? But their responses reveal what they do and do not understand about how all this letter-sound stuff is working. James and Darion do not understand the question. They do not understand that the *word* fire has different sound *parts*. To them the word *fire* is one sound part—fire. For this reason, they do not understand that their teacher is asking them to think about the different *sounds in the word* as opposed to the meaning of the word. So, James thinks about a fire and what sounds a fire might make—crackle. He is not thinking about the *word*. Darion is on the same page in thinking about a fire but he goes to the sounds a person might make if they were telling someone that there was a fire, yelling "Fire!" Again, he also does not understand the question. It's abstract to separate the meaning of the word from its structure—how it is built. However, that's what we are asking children to do when we want them to understand the alphabetic principle.

Tessa understands that her teacher is asking her to talk about the sounds in the word *fire* not the meaning of the word. What she hears, however, is the last and most salient sound /er/ in the word fire, not the beginning sound /f/.

How do we help these children understand the alphabetic principle? Do we tell them, "These letters show the sounds in words?" We could, but that is not likely to be very productive. In fact, we would probably just keep getting the very same responses. Children acquire insights like this when we *show* them and do so repeatedly over time. It might be tempting in this situation to just give up. In fact, we have heard teachers do this, saying, "This is not developmentally appropriate," but this would be a mistake. If you are going to teach letters, then you must teach the alphabet principle and stay the course. Tessa has some insight about the question, and James and Darion just need more exposure. Acquiring the alphabetic principle takes place over time through consistent modeling. They will "get it" with examples, shared reading, interactive writing, listening to peers, and a supportive classroom environment. Thus, the way to help children like James and Darion is to patiently carry on without high pressure and frustration.

The 44 English Phonemes

Our spoken language has different sound units in it. These range from the largest, *word* units, to the smallest, *phonemes* or *speech sounds*. In between words and phonemes are syllables. Syllables are units that consist of a vowel nucleus made by one push of breath (see the Important Terms Table 2.3 below for easy access). Syllables can have consonants at the beginning (e.g., *be, go, me*), end (e.g., *at, egg*), or both (e.g., *leg, bat*) but each syllable must have a vowel sound. Vowels are essential.

A syllable can be broken into an onset and rime (that's the correct spelling; it's a linguistic term). The rime is the vowel and all that comes after it in a syllable and an onset is the consonants that come before the rime (e.g., *wr*-ist, *g*-o, *tr*-ick, *t*-ap). Not all syllables have onsets (e.g. –*it* in hab-it).

The smallest sound unit is the phoneme. Our alphabet is built on speech sounds, phonemes. Teachers must know the phonemes, the basis of the alphabet, what the letters symbolize (See Table 2.2). There are two basic types of sounds: vowels and consonants. A vowel sound is made by opening the vocal track and letting air flow through it. Consonant sounds are made by

Table 2.2 IPA Symbols

Vowels		Consonants	
IPA symbol	Word with sound	IPA symbol	Word with sound
ʌ	h<u>u</u>g	b	<u>b</u>oy
ɑː	<u>a</u>rt	d	<u>d</u>ig
æ	n<u>a</u>p	f	<u>f</u>ish
ə	<u>a</u>way	g	<u>g</u>o
e	g<u>e</u>t	h	<u>h</u>ill
ɜ	f<u>ir</u>, h<u>ur</u>t	j	<u>y</u>es
ɪ	h<u>i</u>t	k	<u>k</u>i<u>c</u>k, <u>c</u>at
i	tr<u>ea</u>t, b<u>e</u>	l	<u>l</u>amp
ɒ	h<u>o</u>t	m	<u>m</u>en
ɔ	l<u>aw</u>	n	<u>n</u>ap
ʊ	b<u>oo</u>k	ŋ	si<u>ng</u>
u	tr<u>ue</u>, f<u>oo</u>d	p	<u>p</u>at
aɪ	n<u>i</u>ce	r	<u>r</u>un
aʊ	n<u>ow</u>	s	<u>s</u>ip
əʊ	t<u>oe</u>	ʃ	<u>sh</u>eet
eə	st<u>air</u>	t	<u>t</u>en
eɪ	d<u>ay</u>	tʃ	<u>ch</u>ick
ɪə	h<u>ear</u>	θ	<u>th</u>ing
ɔɪ	j<u>oi</u>n	ð	<u>th</u>ose
ʊə	t<u>our</u>	v	<u>v</u>et
		w	<u>w</u>oods
		z	<u>z</u>oo
		ʒ	vi<u>si</u>on
		dʒ	lar<u>ge</u>

blocking and releasing or partially restricting air as it moves through the vocal tract. Try to say the following sentence without any vowel sounds: *My mouth does not open if I do not say vowel sounds.* The tongue, teeth, and other parts of the mouth are used to create these sounds. Table 2.2 shows the commonly agreed upon 20 vowel sounds and 24 consonant sounds. The symbols are the International Phonetic Alphabet code. Vowels and consonants differ by how they are made.

Major Letter-Sounds (GPCs) Taught in Early Years

In the preschool years, we teach young children the major letter-sounds (GPCs) associated with the 26 letters and often, the most common consonant digraphs. We will discuss these in three categories, single consonants, vowels, and consonant digraphs. When they are first learning to read, children learn to decode single syllable words, and prior to that, we typically teach the major sounds for single consonants in single syllable words, because these are very regular and usually represent one sound (Gates & Yale, 2011). [Note: For a few letters, there are two sounds.] There is usually one unique sound for the following letters: Bb, Dd, Ff, Hh, Jj, Kk, Ll, Mm, Nn, Pp, Rr, Ss, Tt, Vv, Ww, Yy, and Zz. For Cc and Gg there are both hard sounds (e.g., /g/ as in go and /k/ as in c̠ab) and soft sounds (e.g., Gg representing the soft sound /j/ as in gel and Cc representing the soft /s/ in words where *e* or *i* follow, as in c̠ent). With preschoolers, we prefer to teach the hard sounds /k/ and /g/ for Cc and Gg, but some teachers also teach the soft sounds. Qq and Xx do not represent unique sounds but blends, /ks/ for Xx and /kw/ for Qq. The letter Qq is almost always followed by a Uu (e.g., quest, queen).

With preschoolers, we typically teach both the short and long vowel sounds. The long vowel sounds are those that match the vowel names, and children can easily learn these long sounds. In addition, we teach the short sounds because the single vowels in single-syllable words usually have a short sound (Gates & Yale, 2011). The short sounds are a as in *nap*, e as in *net*, i as in *hit*, o as in *cot*, and u as in *nut*.

A consonant digraph is when two consonants occur together to represent a unique sound (e.g., *ph, th, ch, sh, wh, -ck*). Literally, digraph means two letters written. [Note:. There are also vowel digraphs, such as *oi, oo, oa, ee*, but they are not typically taught until formal reading instruction begins.] The most common and consistent digraphs are *th, ch, sh,* and *wh*. Almost every time you see these two letters together in single syllable words, you will hear the sounds *th*at, *ch*at, *sh*ip, and *wh*en. Increasingly, kindergarten and preschool teachers are actually teaching these four very predictable digraphs, *th, ch, wh,* and *sh*. They are very useful for learning some early high frequency words (e.g., she, when, the).

A consonant blend is two consonants that are adjacent but where each letter retains its own sound (e.g., gr-, tr-, br-, st-, str-, sn-). In the word *frog* you can hear both the sound /f/ and the sound /r/. As discussed in the box *Pictures in Alphabet Charts That Really Help*, when teaching consonants, we use pictures in which the beginning sound in the word is *not* a consonant blend. For example, a picture to cue the sound for Ss, should be words like *sun* and *sail*, not *stream* or *slide*. Young children have difficulty separating the

---

BOX 2.2 Pictures in Alphabet Charts That Really Help (and Ones That Don't!)

In preschool and kindergarten classrooms, teachers use pictures to help remind children of the target sound(s) for a given letter. Unfortunately, some of these pictures confuse children and actually do not help them remember the sounds. Below are some guidelines.

Guideline	Explanation	Non-Example	Example
Is the picture of something that the children know?	If children do not know what the picture is, then the picture will not help to remind them to remember the sound.	"puma"	"cat"
Is the picture clear?	An unclear picture can be uninterpretable and, if so, it cannot remind a child of the sound.	"boat"	"boat"
If for a consonant, does the picture begin with a single consonant and not a digraph or blend?	Children have difficulty isolating a single sound in a consonant blend. In the word *broccoli* they might hear br- as the first sound.	"broccoli"	"banana"
Does the picture have the name of a letter at the beginning?	Some pictures actually repeat the name of a letter at the beginning. For instance, the picture elephant for /e/ has the name of the letter Ll, which can cause confusion.	"elephant" Ll	"egg"

two sounds in a consonant blend and may be confused when these types of words are exemplars. For example, they may identify the beginning sound in *stream* as str- because it is hard to separate those three sounds. In fact, in one study, researchers identified consonant blends as more difficult to decode (Saha, Cutting, Del Tufo, & Bailey, 2021).

Table 2.3 Important Literacy Terms

Important Terms	Meaning
Alphabet	A set of letter symbols representing speech sounds in a word.
Consonant	A speech sound made by restricting, partially or fully, air as it moves through the vocal tract. Single consonants: b-e-d, r-a-t Consonant digraphs: sh-oe, th-at, ch-at Consonant blend: tr-ip, str-eam
consonant digraph	Two adjacent consonants that work together to represent one sound (e.g., sh, th, ch, ph).
consonant blends	Two or more adjacent consonants that are pronounced together but that each retain their unique sounds. For example, you can hear both the /t/ and the /r/ in the blend tr-, as in trip.
grapheme	The letter or letters that represent a phoneme. A grapheme can be one letter, as in the j in *job*, or more than one letter, as in the *sh* in *ship* or the *ee* in *meet*.
grapheme-phoneme correspondences (GPCs)	Visual symbols that represent speech sounds. Sometimes called letter-sound correspondences.
letter	A written, visual symbol used to represent one or more speech sounds.
onset	In a syllable, the consonant, consonant blend or consonant digraph that precedes the vowel. Not all words have onsets (e.g., at). <u>onset</u> <u>rime</u> tr -ip p -et shr -ill

(continued)

Table 2.3 Cont.

Important Terms	Meaning
phoneme	The smallest unit of sound in a language that affects meaning. For example, *bit* and *bat* share two of the same phonemes but differ on a third. The third phoneme influences meaning. to = 2 phonemes (t-o) eight = 2 phonemes (eig-ht) that = 3 phonemes (th-a-t) ax = 3 phonemes (a-k-s)
rime	The part of the syllable (or single-syllable word) that contains the vowel and all that comes after. <u>onset</u> <u>rime</u> s eat br ing t ake j am
syllable	A part of a word that has one vowel sound (e.g., la-dy). Made with one push of breath.
vowel	A speech sound made by opening the vocal tract. All words have vowel sounds in them. Short vowels (also called "lax") are: /a/ van /e/ bet /i/ hit /o/ not /u/ hut Long vowels (also called "tense") are: /a/ ape /e/ eat /i/ ice /o/ open /u/ unicorn

Summary

Every profession has its own jargon and lingo, terms that professionals use as a short-cut to communicate with each other as they do their jobs. Some terms are essential, and others are just part of the lore of a profession. In hospitals, nurses will scream, "Stat!" In restaurants waitstaff will say, "86 on soup of the day," when they mean "out of soup." With early literacy instruction, basic terms like *short vowel, consonant, long vowel,* and *grapheme* are the vocabulary of the profession—the words that teachers use to organize what they are teaching. More than just cool slang, the information in this chapter is essential if we are to teach children the basis of their language. These labels we use create categories that help us as we organize information for children and help them learn. We also find that when teachers think about how writing began, they are better equipped to help young children. Use this chapter as a reference. Flip back when you need to remember something. Mark pages with Post-It notes and make it a reference so that your best time can be spent planning joyful, effective instruction in the classroom.

References

Fillmore, L. W., & Snow, C. E. (2000). What teachers need to know about language. Washington, DC; Office of Educational Research and Improvement.

Gates, L., & Yale, I. (2011). A logical letter-sound system in five phonic generalizations. *The Reading Teacher*, 64(5), 330–339.

Moats, L. C. (2020, June 8). *Teaching reading is rocket science*. American Federation of Teachers. www.aft.org/ae/summer2020/moats

Saha, N. M., Cutting, L. E., Del Tufo, S., & Bailey, S. (2021). Initial validation of a measure of decoding difficulty as a unique predictor of miscues and passage reading fluency. *Reading and Writing*, 34(2), 497–527.

3

Teaching Phonological Awareness

"Research has finally yielded an answer to the question of why learning to use the alphabetic principle is difficult for so many. The impasse lies in the perceptual and conceptual elusiveness of the phonemes."
(Adams, Foorman, Lundberg, & Beeler, 1998)

This is it! This quote, by the authors of an article called *The Elusive Phoneme*, points to one of the main reasons why children may struggle to learn letter-sounds and ultimately become successful readers. If children miss hearing "elusive phonemes" in words, then alphabet instruction will not work. What does this mean specifically? It means that if a child cannot first hear that *ham*, *hit*, and *hug* all start with the /h/ sound, then memorizing letter-names and even letter-sounds (GPCs) is unlikely to lead to applying that knowledge to eventually reading words or spelling. Children must acquire the *insight* that words, apart from their meanings, can be broken into smaller parts and that these parts are symbolically represented in an alphabet. Usually, we cut straight to the symbolic units, the alphabet, without building children's insight about what those symbols are signifying. Children must have an awareness of sounds; this is the foundation upon which alphabet instruction sits.

The ability to hear sound differences in words is pivotal to becoming literate in an alphabetic writing system like English. We call this insight about speech sounds in words phonemic awareness. This chapter will provide some of the basics about phonological and phonemic awareness, what it is, what it is not, why it is important, and how to teach it. Then the chapter will

DOI: 10.4324/9781003130918-3

provide an overview of assessments, a basic scope and sequence for teaching phonemic awareness, and a large set of engaging, fun activities for teaching phonemic awareness including hand motions to use with children.

Basics

Phonological Awareness is Not Phonics

We find that there are four "ph" words that float around in educational circles and typically get confused: *phonics, phonological awareness, phonetics,* and *phonemic awareness* (Figure 3.1). In fact, we confronted this confusion at a recent workshop with teachers. "Phonetics, phonics, phonemic awareness, whatever you want to call it, just tell me how to help kids," requested Tammy, an experienced Head Start teacher. We couldn't agree more with her, but also know that understanding the differences here is critical to effective instruction. It's like differentiating words for children, showing them, for example, that a cow, a dog, and a horse, while all having four legs, are not the same. With these "ph" terms, the unifying thread is "sound." All of these words have the Latin base "phon," which means sound, but they all relate to sound differently.

Phonological awareness is an umbrella term that refers to an awareness of sounds (orally/aurally) in a language. It covers a number of different

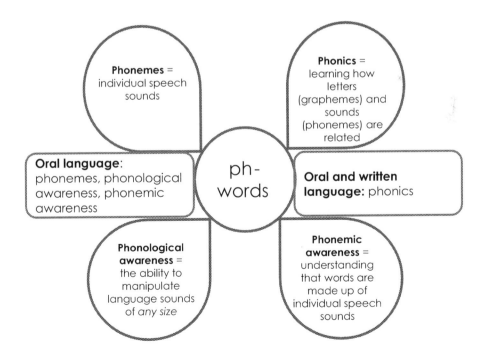

Figure 3.1 Ph Words to Know.

units, large and small, such as words, syllables, rimes, and speech sounds (phonemes). A child who has this type of awareness can tell if two words rhyme, can clap the syllables in a word, and can tell if two words share the same beginning sounds. Phonological awareness is specific to the sounds of language. Thus, it is not the same as distinguishing a clapping hand from a snapping hand or repeating the melody of a song. It is a specific understanding of oral language sounds.

Children do not naturally know where one word ends and the other begins through listening and speaking. We actually do not speak words with "white spaces" between them. We run things together. In fact, children's author Beverly Cleary (1968) illustrates this with her protagonist Ramona Quimby in *Ramona the Pest*, who is learning the lines to the national anthem, "Oh say can you see. By the dawn's early light." Ramona is puzzled: "Next, Miss Binney taught the class the words of a puzzling song about 'the dawnzer lee light,' which Ramona did not understand because she did not know what a dawnzer was." Ramona, having no insight about how the words in the song worked, fused the words *dawn's* and *early*, thinking the two words were one, a *dawnzer*. Later she goes home and tells her parents to turn on the *dawnzer*, the light.

Phonemic awareness is the specific awareness of speech sounds or phonemes, the smallest sound units. It does not include awareness of words, syllables or rime but only refers to speech sounds. It is a type of phonological awareness, the most important type. Phonemic awareness is the specific ability to understand that words are made up of individual speech sounds (i.e., phonemes). Phonemes are the sound pieces of words. For example, *cat* has three sounds. A child with phonemic awareness can identify phonemes (/c/ is at the beginning of cat), break words into phonemes (i.e., "cat" = /c/ /a/ /t/), blend phonemes together to make a word (/c/ + /a/ + /t/ = "cat"), or manipulate phonemes (e.g., "What is *cat* without the /k/ sound?).

Phonemic awareness is important because that is the basis of the alphabetic system in English—letters represent speech sounds or phonemes. If you do not understand that words have these phonemic parts, then you cannot make any sense of "letters making sounds." The alphabetic system makes no sense to you.

What, then, is *phonics?* Like *phonological awareness, phonemic awareness,* and *phonetics,* the word *phonics* has the *phon* word root, meaning sound. Phonics is teaching readers the association between letters (graphemes) and sounds (phonemes) to support them in decoding. Phonics deals with written language, and phonemic awareness deals with oral language. Phonics you see, in letters, and hear, in phonemes. Phonemic awareness deals with oral language, with the main focus being hearing and orally working with sounds.

Phonemic Awareness Front Loads Letter-Sound Instruction Particularly for At-Risk Students

We know that phonemic awareness is an essential part of any preschool curriculum, and that a robust line of research supports it (Ehri et al., 2001; National Reading Panel Report, 2000; Suggate, 2016). We believe that the research can be boiled down to three important points for teachers. First, phonemic awareness instruction is important because it primes or "front loads" later phonics instruction (Lundberg, Frost, & Peterson, 1988). If children understand sounds in words, they are going to be more receptive to later learning letter-sounds (GPCs) and then even later, decoding words. If you do not understand that *lamp* and *like* start with the sound /l/, then learning the letter symbol Ll and the sound will make little sense to you.

Second, we know that many children who struggle to learn to read lack phonemic awareness (Juel, 1988). In other words, they cannot retain "phonics" instruction because they do not understand the entire system. Now, some children, usually those with a precocious gift for language, figure it out with adult modeling and a few examples, but this is not reliable for the majority of children (Castles, Rastle, & Nation, 2018).

In fact, this leads to our third point; researchers found in a review of programs for struggling readers that phonemic awareness training had better long-term effects than phonics. In other words, high quality phonemic awareness training helped children the most, especially over time. Others agree—phonemic awareness is very important for students at higher risk of reading difficulties and should be a part of early education (Kilpatrick, 2015; Shaywitz, 2003).

The reason that we care about phonemic awareness instruction is because it builds capacity for sounding out and spelling words once we add letters.

Best Practices in Phonological Awareness Instruction

We know much about how to deliver effective phonological awareness instruction. In the 1990s, researchers established that, for many children, the "missing link" in terms of reaching literacy is lack of awareness of the sound structure in our alphabetic language. The National Reading Panel (2000), and the National Early Literacy Panel report about ten years later, reviewed dozens of instructional studies. These studies deliver some important points about instruction, as summarized below. Phonemic awareness instruction:

- should be developmentally appropriate
- should be lively and engaging, matching the natural language play that children enjoy
- is often most effective in small groups where teacher feedback and attention are high
- should not be lengthy; for young children 10–20 minutes is ideal
- should follow a scope and sequence
- should be taught in coordination with letter instruction

The last point, about coordinating with letter instruction, is often misunderstood. Some teachers believe that this means they should always introduce letters *as they are teaching* phonemic awareness (Kirkpatrick, 2015). In fact, many of the early studies reviewed by the NRP consisted of daily instructional approaches lasting for weeks that never introduced letters or followed PA instruction with letter instruction. This was necessary in order to clearly establish that PA instruction caused improvements in literacy. However, in today's classrooms, PA instruction includes letters but may also immediately precede or follow letter instruction. We find that preschoolers often benefit from a PA "warm-up" with five to seven minutes of oral PA instruction without letters and then immediately after, with no time break, letter instruction based on the sounds targeted in PA. It is important and useful, especially with preschoolers, to initially work with sounds ahead of letters. Letters will always be connected with PA instruction, but sometimes doing one thing at a time works well.

Sounds: Larger Units, "Stretchable" Sounds, and Fewer Sounds are Easiest

"Whew! That's a lot that you're laying on me! I mean, I can do all kinds of fun things with language play. I don't really need these fancy terms!" exclaimed one teacher in a recent meeting. Yes, we have added a number of terms here. However, we would argue that this is the language of professional educators and it is used in every curriculum and standards document for preschoolers. Teachers should understand this language. Overcomplicating anything does not make it more effective. However, prior to getting down to the engaging and joyful phonological awareness activities, most teachers need to organize three aspects of sound in their minds:

- sizes of sound units (words vs. syllables vs. phonemes)
- types of sounds they are asking children to analyze (continuants vs. stops)
- number of sounds (two vs. three)

Size of Sound Units

As shown in Figure 3.2, we can work with sound units that are different sizes. In general, we know that children become aware of larger sound units prior to smaller units (Anthony et al., 2002; Liberman et al., 1974), moving from words to syllables to onsets/rimes to the beginning and final sounds of words and finally to each phoneme in a word. Thus, when we do phonological awareness instruction, we start with larger units first. For example, once children can clap or tap the number of syllables in a word (el-e-phant), they are usually ready to separate the onset from the rime in single-syllable words (e.g., th-at, t-oe, c-at, str-ip). After this work of breaking onsets and rimes, work can focus on matching words with the same first sound, naming the initial sound, or saying a word with the same beginning sound. The last and most challenging unit is working with individual speech sounds or phonemes. An example might be when we give a child a series of sounds and ask them to blend them into a word (e.g., /d/ /o/ /g/ = dog) or, even harder, when we ask them to break down a word (e.g., mit = /m/ /i/ /t/).

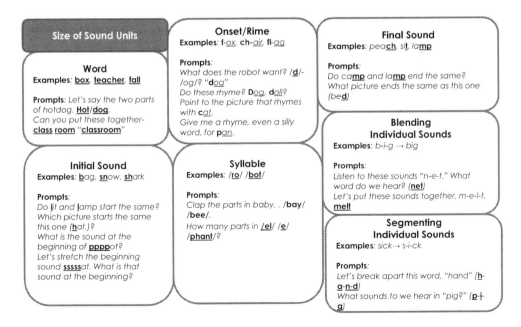

Figure 3.2 Types of Sound Units.

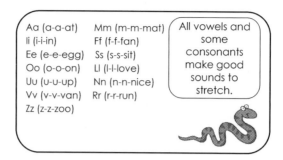

Figure 3.3 Good Stretchable Sounds to Start With.

Types of Sounds (Easy to Stretch vs. Hard to Stretch)

Another aspect that influences instructional difficulty is the type of sound. Any teacher who has worked with individual speech sounds knows that some sounds are easy to stretch out and others are not. Any vowel sound can be articulated and held as long as the person has breath (e.g., aaaaaat, iiiin). Certain consonant sounds (e.g., mmmmmat, lllllllip) can also be stretched for a long time. However, other consonant sounds, such as /g/ (go) cannot be stretched. The only way to make the sound /g/ go on and on is to keep saying it over and over /g/ /g/ /g/. We call the stretchable sounds continuants because they can be continued (see Figure 3.3 for a listing of these). When they begin blending and segmenting sounds, most teachers like to start with vowel and continuant consonant sounds first.

Number of Sounds

Thirdly, we pay attention to how many sounds we are asking children to work with, because more sounds place a higher burden on children cognitively. Let's explain. In one study that Heidi Anne conducted, she asked students to repeat the sentence orally, "*Fruit salad has peaches and oranges.*" She was asking them to remember six words with over nine syllables. Unfortunately, a number of three- and four-year-olds did not have the verbal memory to remember all those words. Sentences came out, "peaches and oranges," or "fruit salad and oranges."

The same happens with phonemes or speech sounds if we ask children to remember three sounds as opposed to two. Sometimes, with segmenting sounds, a child will "lose" the first sounds. For example, if a teacher said, "Can you break *cat* into three sounds?" the child could respond with "Ca-t," fusing the beginning consonant and vowel. The reason is likely because there are three sounds in the word *cat*. Instead of asking this student to break down a three-sound word, the teacher could ask them to break down a two-sound word like *at, see,* or *ate* (note that the number of sounds in a word and the number of letters is not always the same). When we are doing phonemic awareness training, we focus on the *sounds*, so if a word has three letters but only two sounds, it is a good word for segmenting and blending. Breaking words into two sounds makes the task easier because there are only two units to work with. If we are moving to asking children to blend sounds together, we might start with words that only have two sounds. Below is another example of a blending and segmenting lesson with only two sounds.

Teacher *Let's see what Pop, our puppet, is trying to say. What is this word? m-ow?*
Child: *mow.*
Teacher: *What about this word? S-ay?*
Child: *say.*
　　Then we would move to segmenting two phoneme words:
Teacher: *What are the sounds in go?*
Child: */g/ /o/.*

Cues and Tasks: What Children Do with Sounds Influences Lesson Difficulty

Teachers need to pay attention to what they are asking children to do with sounds (task demands) (Anthony et al., 2002; Morais, 1991; Muter et al., 1997; Wagner et al., 1994). This is the nitty-gritty of instruction, the modeling that we give, the questions that we ask, and the kinds of answers that we expect of children. All requests and tasks are not created equally. We outline three different types of cues—oral, physical, and visual—that make sounds concrete for young children. We also describe the following task considerations when working with preschoolers, including answers that are receptive versus expressive, and activity types that require matching, identifying the "odd one," isolation, blending, and segmenting.

Oral, Physical, and Visual Cues

Instructional cues are the prompts or props that bring focus to sounds and make them more noticeable and concrete for preschoolers. These prompts can be oral, visual, or physical. Sometimes cues are just oral, repeating or emphasizing a target sound such as when a teacher does a silly rhyming circle: "Let's each say silly words that rhyme with *day* ... *fay, nay, lay, may, shay.*" Repetitive alliteration games and tongue twisters are similar: "Peter Piper picked a peck of pickled peppers," because the oral cue is the most prominent—hearing the repeated sound orally is what makes this work.

　　With young children, physical/kinesthetic cues are very powerful. Teachers can ask children to clap the two parts of a compound word or take a step for each syllable of a word or jump for each word they hear. Hand signals are very popular and are used in many programs, including Heggerty and Orton–Gillingham. We offer a series of hand signals for different types of activities below, but many teachers invent their own.

Of course, visual cues like chips or unifix blocks are also very effective because these offer a visual prop to make sounds concrete and real. Children can use unifix cubes to "break" a two-phoneme word orally as they physically separate cubes. Lastly, phonemic awareness instruction will move towards using letters as visual cues, but only as children are learning these.

Tasks: Receptive versus Expressive, Oddity, Isolation, and Segmenting

Tasks also influence instruction or how we ask students to respond to a PA question. This is a big part of what makes instruction hard or easy. Receptive tasks are easier than expressive tasks (see Table 3.1: Types of Tasks, what are they and what do they look like?). A receptive task is when a teacher asks a child to listen and then make a response, by pointing, choosing, nodding, or giving a "thumbs up." Receptive answers do not require the child to say or express a sound or answer. For instance, a teacher asks a child, "Which has the same beginning as bbboy, bbbat, bbbig?" and then waits for the child to point to the "bear." In this situation, the child is responding but does not have to tell the teacher the sound he hears is /b/.

Expressive tasks require children to not only hear or detect a difference or similarity but to go one-step further and say a sound part. One example might be a teacher asking, "What sound do you hear at the beginning of ssssip?" to which the child must reply /s/. Another example would be a teacher saying "Let's clap the syllables in ba-by. Now you do it, ba-by. What's the first part in ba-by?" to which the child would reply "ba-."

Teachers can also select tasks that require matching, oddity, isolation, blending, and segmenting. Matching and oddity tasks are often done at the beginning of instruction because they seize on children's emerging insights about sound. When matching, children find items, pictures, or make oral choices around "same sounds," or "words that are like___." For instance, "Find the picture that has the same rhyme as 'man' [bag, shoe, fan.]" or "Listen. Which word starts like bbbbboy? bbbbbat, tttttail?" Oddity tasks similarly seize on emerging intuition by asking children, "Which one does *not* fit?" This item, for example, focuses on rhyme, "Which one is different— h<u>a</u>t? j<u>og</u>? b<u>a</u>t?"

In order to connect letters to phonemes, children must be able to isolate sounds, particularly at the beginning of words. They must be able to find, say, or match beginning sounds in order to go to the next step and then attach a visual symbol to a speech sound. Think of it this way: a child who does not have the insight that /h/ is the beginning sound in *hat* will not make sense

Table 3.1 Types of Tasks, What Are They, and What Do They Look Like?

Task	What is it?	What does it look like?
Oddity	Being able to discriminate sounds or detect differences.	Which one does not sound the same "big, fig, hat?" Which one does not sound the same "sssssat, bbbboy, ssssoap?"
Matching	Being able to discriminate sounds or detect differences.	Find the picture with the same sound at the beginning as "ddddog." Find the one that rhymes with "cap." Match the pictures with the same first sound.
Generating/Producing	The ability to create or make a sound.	Say the first sound in "baby." (Isolate) Say a word that rhymes with "boy." Say the first part of "bub-ble."
Blending	The ability to connect individual speech sounds.	What word do these sounds make? "dddd-ad" or "mmm-ooo-mmmm."
Segmenting	The ability to break words into individual speech sounds.	Here's the word "sun." What sounds do we hear in "sun?"
Manipulating	The ability to take off, put on, or change sounds.	Say "football." Now say it without "foot." Say "fox." Now say it with /b/ at the beginning.

of the teacher telling her, "Hh makes the sound /h/." Now she may learn to articulate /h/ during circle time when the teacher points to Hh and all her friends are around, and she may even learn to say /h/ when her teacher points to the Hh, but she will not really know how to use that information. Initial sound knowledge is the threshold, the turning point. If a child cannot find, say, or match beginning sounds, alphabet instruction is pointless.

After children can identify and isolate particular types of sounds, they are usually ready to blend or put together sounds and then later segment or break up sounds (Wagner et al., 1994). When a child blends sounds, they hear them pronounced separately and then put them together, like this, "Robby Robot says words in funny ways, like 'hot-dog' when he means 'hotdog.' What word is he trying to say, 'pan-cake?'" Here is another example, "What word is this /g/ /e/ /t/?" Keep in mind that in blending tasks you are giving the children the parts and asking them to fuse them together.

Segmenting is the opposite of blending. This is giving children the whole and then asking them to break it into parts. You can see how this is harder. The child has to analyze and have an understanding of the sound parts in the activity. For instance, "Here's the word *at*. What are the sounds in *at*?" Some children will catch on to segmenting just from hearing the teacher do it, and other times more support is needed. Teachers will make the sounds concrete by used hand signals, like "chopping" the word, tapping their arms, or holding up fingers for each sound. Often teachers will slowly say the sounds in a word to emphasize the parts.

Manipulating phonemes is the most difficult task for students and is not typically part of a preschool curriculum. In fact, many preschool teachers may not even "get to" segmenting or blending because they can be over the heads of many preschoolers. When we ask children to manipulate, we ask them to take off, put on, or change sounds. For example, "Say *hotdog*. Now say it without *hot*." Now say *hot* with /f/ at the beginning. *fot*." As you can tell, these are complex, multistep activities. To separate *hot* from *dog* the child must first hear the two parts, then separate them, and finally identify the one requested. These skills actually are most effectively taught with letters (NRP, 2000). Letters provide a cognitive storage mechanism for manipulating phonemes; indeed, that is what spelling words is.

Scope and Sequence for Daily Phonological Awareness

This scope and sequence provides a guide for structuring your phonological awareness instruction and move from larger units and easier tasks to smaller units and more challenging tasks. The guide is not meant to be rigid. We want you to use the knowledge you have regarding your students in addition to this framework to create an instructional plan that works for you. Each focus or new skill should be introduced for about three weeks. The early units are for younger three-year-olds and the later units are for four-year-olds. The focus sound unit is listed, but keep in mind that the tasks can make it more or less difficult. For example, there are a number of rhyme activities, but the

Table 3.2 Phonological Awareness Scope and Sequence

Target Age	Unit #/New Skill (three weeks/unit)	Teacher says …	Child can …	Skills to Review
Early three-year-olds	**1. Rhyme (Listen)** Hearing rhymes in literature. Participating in nursery rhymes or other poems.	We will sing this nursery rhyme together today. (Emphasize the rhymes in the song.) Twinkle, twinkle, little **star**/ How I wonder what you **are**/ Up above the world so **high**/ Like a diamond in the **sky**/	Recite nursery rhymes and/or poems with the teacher and class.	
	2. Words Identifying words in a short sentence. (Expressive/Producing)	What makes a word different from a sentence? What words make up the sentence? I/love/you Reading/is/fun (Use fingers to show each word.)	With teacher support, the child can identify individual words in a sentence. I/love/you Reading/is/fun (Use fingers to show each word.)	Listening and participating in rhymes

(continued)

Table 3.2 Cont.

Target Age	Unit #/New Skill (three weeks/unit)	Teacher says …	Child can …	Skills to Review
Early three-year-olds	3. Word vs. Sound Word versus Beginning Sound: what's the difference?	What is a word? fun What is a sound? /f/ How are they different?	Identify words and beginning sounds. Word: fun Sound: /f/ Words are made up of sounds. Sounds are usually shorter than words.	Listening and participating in rhymes. With teacher support the child can identify individual words in a sentence.
	4. Rhyme (Naming) Name a word that rhymes with a target.	Tell me a word that sounds like cat? bat/sat/dat ___ ? (Silly words are fine!)	Bat, sat, dat, hat, fat … (Silly words are fine!)	With teacher support, the child can identify individual sounds in words.
	5. Words (Blends) Blending compound words	Listen to the words *rain* and *bow*. If we put those together, what do we make? Rain-bow → rainbow	When we put together rain and bow, we make rainbow. (Use fists for each part and put together.)	Name a word that rhymes with a target.

Early four-year-olds	Late three-yr-olds			
		6. Words (Segment) Segmenting compound words	Let's take this word apart. Icecream. What are the two words? icecream → ice-cream Use the segmenting hand motion (stacking) below.	We hear ice and cream. (Use fists, start with them together and then move apart for each word.)	Blend a compound word (hot-dog). Name a word that rhymes with a target.
		7. Rhyme (Odd one out) Identify the non-rhyming word. Which one doesn't match?	Listen to these words. Which sound different at the end? Easier (different vowels) hit, hat, mat Harder (same vowels) hog, log, hop	Hit does not rhyme. Hop does not rhyme.	Segment a compound (starfish = star-fish).
		8. Rhyme (Match) Match words by rhyme.	Which of these words rhyme? Can you match them with the words that sound the same? bag, wet, net, tag	Bag and tag sound the same AND net and wet sound the same (rhyme).	Identifying non-rhyming words. Which one does not belong?

(continued)

Table 3.2 Cont.

Target Age	Unit #/New Skill (three weeks/unit)	Teacher says …	Child can …	Skills to Review
Late three-year-olds / Early four-year-olds	9. Syllables (Blend) Blend syllables into a word	Listen to the word parts o-pen. If we put those together, what word do we make? O-pen → open	If we put together o-pen, we make the word open. (Use fists or other hand movements to show putting together.)	Match the words that rhyme. big, hat, fig, bat
	10. Syllables (Segment) Segment words into syllables.	How many word parts do you hear? What parts do you hear? Basic → ba-sic Use the segmenting hand motion (stacking) below.	Basic. We hear (or clap) two parts, /ba/ and /sic/	Blend syllables into a word. Match the words that rhyme. big, hat, fig, bat

Teaching Phonological Awareness ◆ 49

		11. Onset/Rime (Blending) Blending onset and rime to create a word. *this looks similar to syllable blending, but here we are blending onset/rime.	Listen to the word parts m-en. If we blend those together, what word do we make? m-en → men Use the onset/rime hand motion below.	When we put together m-en, we make the word men.	Blend and segment words into syllables. la-dy = lady candy = can-dy
Late four-year-olds		12. Onset/Rime (Segmenting) Segmenting onset/rime using the initial sound. *this looks similar to syllable segmenting, but here we are segmenting onset/rime.	What is the first part of men (onset)? s-it What is the rest of s-it (rime)? sit→ s-it Use the segmenting hand motion (stacking) below.	When we break apart *sit*, we first hear /s/ and then /it/.	Blend onset and rime. m-en = men.
	Sounds: Identifying beginning sounds is the most important skill and directly supports learning letter-sounds. Teach to mastery before going on to skills below.					

(*continued*)

Table 3.2 Cont.

Target Age	Unit #/New Skill (three weeks/unit)	Teacher says …	Child can …	Skills to Review
	13. Sounds (Beginning) Identify the first sound in a word.	What sound do you hear at the beginning of this word? Fish	We hear /f/	Segment onsets and rimes. sit = /s/ /it/.
	NOTE: Do not proceed to skills below until children are able to identify beginning sounds.			
Late four-year-olds	14. Sounds (Blending 2) Blend two-sound words by phoneme.	Listen to the sounds /e/ /g/. If we blend those together, what word do we make? /e/ /gg/ → egg	When we put together /e/ /g/, we make the word egg	Identify the first sound in a word. l-et = /l/
	15. Sounds (Segment 2) Segment two-sound words by phoneme.	Let's listen for individual sounds. What sounds do you hear at the beginning of bee? End? bee → /b/ /ee/ Use the segmenting hand motion (stacking) below.	When we break apart bee, we first hear /b/ then /ee/ /b/ /ee/	Blend two-sound words by phoneme. /a/ /t/ = at.

Teaching Phonological Awareness ♦ 51

Late four-year-olds (Optional)	Remember to find words with two *sounds*. The number of letters and the number of sounds may not be the same. Many words with three letters have only two sounds (bee, say, toe).			
	16. Sounds (Blend 3) Blend three-sound words by phoneme.	Listen to the sounds /l/ /igh/ /t/. If we blend those together, what word do we make? /l/ /igh/ /t/ → light	When we put together /l/ /igh/ /t/, we make the word light.	Blend three-sound words. /l/ /igh/ /t/ = light.
	17. Sounds (Segment 3) Segment three-sound words by phoneme.	Let's listen for individual sounds. What sounds do you hear at the beginning of dog? Middle? End? dog → /d/ /o/ /g/ Use the segmenting hand motion (stacking) below.	When we break apart dog, we first hear /d/ then /o/ /g/.	Segment two-sound words by phoneme. go = /g/ /o/

first is just exposure, the next is producing a rhyme (even a silly word), then finding the non-rhyming word that does not fit (oddity), and finally matching groups of words that rhyme (e.g., cat, bag, tag, hat, mat). Blending sounds (words, syllables, sounds) is easier and always comes before segmenting or breaking up sounds. The review that is paired with the new skills is a way to spiral back to skills taught in previous weeks and will help prepare your students for the next focus topic. In some situations, harder review skills are repeated several times. Remember that phonological awareness instruction is focused on the sounds, so should not require the child to be reading or writing sounds or words.

Assessments for Phonological Awareness

We find that children may have some natural insights about sounds, insights that they have mastered intuitively. For this reason, it is a good idea to do a simple phonological awareness assessment (See Figure 3.4). This simple one that we have put together is all done **orally,** and it has a range of sound units and tasks starting with larger units and simpler tasks and moving to smaller units and more difficult tasks. The first two sections focus on rhyme, with the first section requiring the child to recognize rhyme and the second section requiring the child to say a rhyming word. The middle section requires the child to identify the beginning sound in a word, a skill commonly thought to be essential for learning letter-sounds. If you have a child who is not retaining letter-sounds that you have taught, this part of the assessment will let you know if phonemic awareness is the problem. This section also has a part on listening for ending sounds. The last section involves blending and segmenting sounds, a skill that is related to decoding. Blending is the easier skill and segmenting the more difficult. Both sections have two- and three-phoneme words, with the two-phoneme words being the easiest.

Phonological Awareness Assessment

Teacher Directions

Materials:
- teacher direction pages
- teacher recording tables
- optional: counting chips or other small manipulative

Directions:
Directions for each subtest are on the following pages. Begin with the Rhyme assessment and move on to the Sounds Part I and II assessments.
If a student reaches frustration (0/4 correct) stop assessment.

Results:
A score of 8/8 (4/4 in an individual section) suggests the child has a good understanding of the concept. A score of 0-2 (out of 8) or 0-1 (out of 4), suggests that the child has minimal knowledge and is perhaps not ready for instruction in that area yet. A score of 3-6 (out of 8) or 2-3 (out of 4) suggests that the child is beginning to understand the concept but requires further instruction in that area.

Note: Concept of Word should also be assessed as a part of phonological awareness, see separate assessment for this.

Phonological Awareness Directions

Rhymes

Recognition

Model for the child. "Words that share the same ending sound, rhyme. Dog, frog, hog, and jog all rhyme. Let's rhyme together. I will tell you 2 words and you tell me if they rhyme. _sit - fit_." If child answers correctly, say "Good, let's try some more." If child gives incorrect answer, help by providing the correct response and restate what a rhyme is.

"Let's do some more. I will tell you two words and you tell me if they rhyme." Read the below sets of words. Record the child's response (check correct).

| 1. jet - pet | 3. car - cat |
| 2. red - ran | 4. bug - hug |

Production

"Now you get to make up the rhyming word. I will tell you a word and you will tell me a word that rhymes. It can be a real word or a made up one!"

"Let's try one together. pig, fig (pause) jig, mig. It's ok to say silly, made-up words."

"Now you try. I'll say a word and you tell me a word that rhymes. dog." (pause for child to respond). If child responds correctly, say "Good, let's make some more rhymes." If they respond incorrectly, provide the correct response and restate the task.

"Let's make some more rhymes. I will tell you a word and you tell me a word that rhymes with it." Read the below set of words. Record child responses.

| 1. bag | 3. dad |
| 2. rub | 4. nut |

Phonological Awareness Directions

Sounds Part I

Initial Sounds

"I am going to read a few words. We are listening for the first sound in the words. If I say moon, you will tell me /m/ because the first sound in moon is mmmm." Make sure child knows to tell you the sound and not the letter name.

"Let's try one. What sound do you hear at the start of big?" /b/
If child provides the incorrect response, assist them by using the language in the first prompt.
If child provides the correct response, continue.

"Now let's try some more." Read the sets of words below. Record the child's response.

| 1. hat - hill | 3. money - map |
| 2. dog - duck | 4. look - line |

Ending Sounds

"I am going to read a few words. This time, we are listening for the last sound in the words. If I say sun, you will tell me /n/ because the sound at the end of sun is nnnn." Make sure child knows to tell you the sound and not the letter name.

"Let's try one. What sound do you hear at the end of mat?" /t/
If child provides the incorrect response, assist them by using the language in the first prompt.
If child provides the correct response, continue.

"Now let's try some more." Read the sets of words below. Record the child's response.

| 1. green | 3. fall |
| 2. foot | 4. good |

Figure 3.4 Phonological Awareness Assessment Preview (the assessment can be found in its entirety in Appendix A).

Figure 3.4 Cont.

Phonological Awareness Directions		
Sounds Part II		
Segmenting	"I am going to tell you a word and you are going to break the sounds apart. If I say dog, I want you to say /d/ /o/ /g/." (You may use counting chips to demonstrate, allowing the child to touch or slide one for each sound they hear-demonstrate for the child) "Let's try one. jam Can you pull the sounds apart?" /j/ /a/ /m/ If child response is incorrect, guide in understanding the task and provide the correct response. If correct, move on to attempt more words. "Now let's try a few more. I will tell you a word and you will break it apart to tell me each sound you hear." Continue with word set below and record student responses.	
	1. egg	3. ape
	2. bat	4. pan
Blending	"Now I will tell you some sounds and you are going to put them together to make a word. If I say /r/ /a/ /t/ then you will say rat. " "Let's try one. /f/ /a/ /n/. Can you put the sounds together?" fan If child response is incorrect, guide in understanding the task and provide the correct response. If correct, move on to attempt more words. "Now let's try a few more. I will tell you a word and you will put it together to make a word." Continue with word set below and record student responses.	
	1. /b/ /ee/	3. /v/ /a/ /n/
	2. /t/ /a/ /g/	4. /z/ /i/ /p/

Phonological Awareness Recording Page				
Student Name: _____ Date Assessed: _____				
Rhymes				
Recognition	jet - pet		car - cat	
	red - ran		bug - hug	/4
Production	bag		dad	
	rub		nut	/4
Subtotal				/8
Sounds Part I				
Initial	hat - hill		money - map	
	dog - duck		look - line	/4
Final	green		fall	
	foot		good	/4
Subtotal				/8
Sounds Part II				
Segment	egg (e-gg)		ape (a-pe)	
	bat (b-a-g)		pan (p-a-n)	/4
Blend	/b/ /ee/ (bee)		/v/ /a/ /n/ (van)	
	/t/ /a/ /g/ (tag)		/z/ /i/ /p/ (zip)	/4
Subtotal				/8

Activities and Games for Phonological Awareness

Hand Motions

Onset/Rime: As you say the word, grab/catch the onset in one hand and then grab/catch the rime with the other (See Figure 3.5).

"stay"   st   ay

Figure 3.5 Onset/Rime.

Segmenting Sound Units (syllables, compound words, onset/rime, or phonemes): Use fists to stack each sound unit (See Figure 3.6).

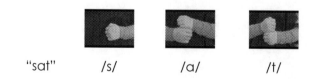

"sat"   /s/   /a/   /t/

Figure 3.6 Segmenting Sound Units.

Blending Two Parts: Stack your fists to add each sound and pull/stretch out the word (See Figure 3.7).

f-ill   fill

Figure 3.7 Blending Two Parts.

Rhyming

Dramatized Rhymes: Introduce a nursery rhyme and then use picture and/or sound supports to read it again (e.g., pictures of a clock and mice, sound of a clock for "Hickory Dickory Dock"). Then, introduce motions that match the rhyme. These should be simple motions that the child could do themselves (e.g., having the children pretend to eat curds and whey in "Little Miss Muffet"). Following the dramatization, explore additional rhyming words (Roush, 2005).

Pass the Rhyme: Prepare this activity by placing an assortment of objects in a bucket. Provide a word that rhymes with one of the objects (real or made up) (See Figure 3.8). Have the children select an object that rhymes with your word. For example, if you want the child to select "glue" from the bucket, ask, "What rhymes with shoe (or blue, crew, moo …)?" and the child will hold up glue from the bucket.

Ball → "Fall"

Figure 3.8 Pass the Rhyme.

Draw and Erase: Prepare by drawing a picture on a chalk or dry erase board that includes a variety of objects (e.g., a farm scene) (See Figure 3.9). Say a word (e.g., bat) and ask a child to come erase the word that rhymes with it. The child will erase the picture that rhymes (e.g., cat rhymes with bat). This could also be done in reverse, having the child add to the picture a word that rhymes with a word you provide.

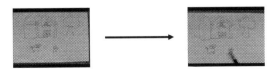

Figure 3.9 Draw and Erase.

Match It: You will need to prepare a set of images that have pairs that rhyme (e.g., bat and cat). Children will match the cards to their rhyming words. This can be set up using a pocket chart with pre-placed images (e.g., set "wig" in the chart and have the child find and place "pig" next to it) or it can be played as a matching memory type game.

Words

Sound Detectives: As sound detectives, students will practice listening for sounds in their environment. This will help them learn to listen for sounds as you begin to introduce them to words and word sounds. Students will use their ears to listen for sounds in their environment. Students find a comfortable spot in the room (or outside), and you explain that they are going to be detectives listening for sounds and will want to stay in their spot for about five minutes for some "detective time." Ask them to close their eyes and listen for sounds in the room. What they hear of course depends on your classroom; maybe squeaky shoes in the hallway, a dripping faucet, or a sneeze, just to name a few. As the lead detective, you help them discuss and share their sounds.

Who Said That? Students sit or stand in a circle, and one child is picked to be in the middle as the "special listener." The special listener closes their eyes (or you can find a fun eye mask to wear) and puts on their "sound listening ears." Choose another child to make an animal noise (e.g., moo, baa, neigh). The special listener has to guess by pointing which direction the animal sound is coming from. This helps prepare the children for listening to sounds more closely in words. Switch roles and allow each child to have a chance in each role.

Counting Chips: Counting chips are useful for a range of phonological awareness activities. In this example, use chips to guide children in counting the number of words in a sentence (See Figure 3.10). Create a frame like the

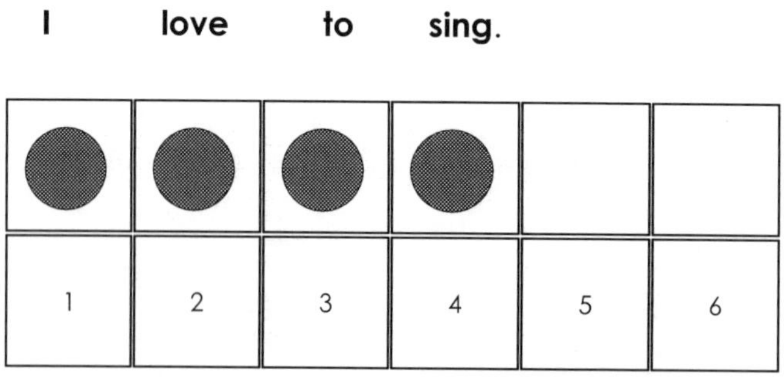

Figure 3.10 Counting Chips.

one pictured below and gather counting chips. Use the counters to count the words in a single sentence by placing or pushing each one into a box as you say the sentence. To start, use sentences with only three to four words and mostly single syllable words, such as "I love my dog" and supply the correct number of chips. Ask children to move each chip into the box as they say each word in the sentence. Move on to more complex sentences, "My brother likes to ride bikes." The fewer function words used (e.g., a, the, to, for) the easier. Try to keep sentences no longer than six words.

Syllables

Handclap Games. These are fun for students and low preparation level for teachers, making them easy to incorporate. One commonly used example is *Bippity Boppity Bumblebee*. Students sit in a circle and the teacher asks one child, "Bippity Boppity Bumble Bee, Will You Say Your Name For Me?" The child says their name, "Martin." The teacher then asks, "Let's say it together" and the students clap the syllables together as they repeat the name, "Mar-tin." The teacher and class together then say, "Bippity Boppity Bumble Bee, Thank You For Saying Your Name For Me!" They can repeat using different volume levels (loud, whisper) to mix it up a little or if students are familiar, a student can become the "teacher" and lead. This can be made more fun by passing around a stuffed animal version of a bumblebee to denote who's turn it is.

Picture This: This activity requires you to have photos of the students in your class, as well as a pocket chart. Print photos of each child in the class to be used as sorting cards. It may be good to laminate these so they can be used multiple times. The children will pick up a picture and say the name of the person on it out loud. They will count the syllables using claps or hand motions and place the picture under the number that matches it (See Figure 3.11). For

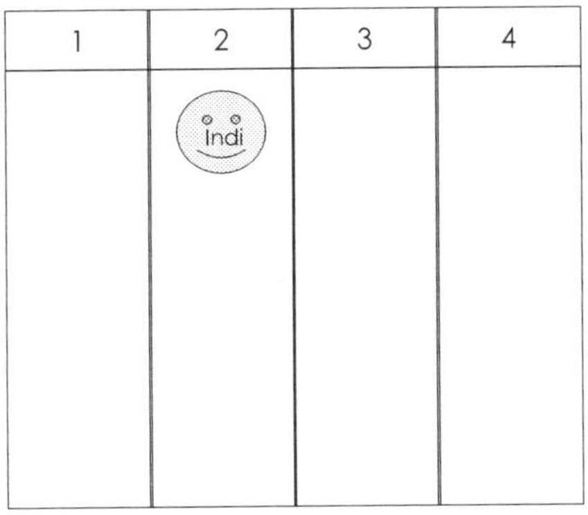

1	2	3	4
	Indi		

Figure 3.11 Picture This.

example, a child picks up a picture of Indi, they clap In-di and then place her picture under the number 2 on the chart.

Bunny Hop: We love getting our students up and moving. In this activity, the children will pretend to be little bunnies who want to hop, hop, hop. Each bunny gets a picture card that you have prepared ahead of time. They are only allowed to hop as many hops as the number of syllables on their picture card. For example, if a child selects a picture of a dinosaur, they would hop up and down three times saying, "di-no-saur, three." You can make this a race or play as a whole group as well.

Initial Sounds

I Spy or Scavenger Hunt: The teacher leads the students in a hunt for objects that begin with a specific sound. For example, go to the playground and look for words that begin with /m/ and students may say "monkey bars" or "mulch." This can be done using pictures of objects hung in the classroom or on a paper to circle as well.

Sensory Bin: The teacher will find small objects to place in a rice or sand sensory bin. Students will search for items and as they pull them out, they will say the sound the object begins with. For example, if they pull out a fish from the bin, the child should say "/f/."

Sound Sorting Cups: This activity also uses small objects, such as a small dinosaur, coins, or buttons, as well as cups or small buckets that are labeled with pictures (not just letters as we are focusing on letter-sounds, not names). Children will sort the objects into the cups based on the beginning sound. For example, if the child pulls out a button, they would place it in the container with the bear on it as each of the words begin with the sound /b/. We recommend only including objects with 2–3 different beginning sounds to sort into 2–3 cups.

Name Game: This is a song to the tune of Old MacDonald, but it can be chanted as well. The teacher asks, "What is the sound that starts these words? Matthew, Mommy, Muck" and the children respond, "Mmmmm is the sound that starts those words, Matthew, Mommy, Muck." Any words can be used as an example; we like using student names. Be aware that the child response should be the word sound, /m/ in our example, and not the letter name.

Segmenting/Blending

Rubber Band Stretch: Prepare the rubber bands (see Figure 3.12 for an example) by placing a sticky note for each individual sound in the word (or word parts if practicing segmenting syllables or compound words) and placing them on the rubber band. Students use the bands to stretch the word apart into individual sounds.

Teaching Phonological Awareness ◆ 59

Figure 3.12 Rubber Band Stretch.

Stepping Stones: Place three or four stepping stones in an area where children can jump in the classroom or outdoors. Either say a word or have a student select a picture card from a bag. As the child segments the word, they jump on each "stone." For example, if the word bat was selected, the child would jump three times, saying "b-a-t, bat." You could also draw lily pads and be frogs jumping or astronauts jumping on footprints on the moon to change up the theme of the activity.

Visual Props: Using chips or unifix blocks as a visual prop can help make sounds concrete and real. Children can use unifix cubes to "break" a two-phoneme word orally as they physically separate cubes (See Figure 3.13). Children can place chips to represent each sound they are identifying (individual sounds, word parts, words).

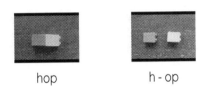

hop   h - op

Figure 3.13 Visual Props.

Chapter Summary

In his book *The Reading Mind*, cognitive psychologist Daniel Willingham (2017) tells us that when children learn letter-sounds (GPCs) there are three pieces of information they must master: 1) visually discriminating one letter from another (e.g., b versus d), 2) becoming aware of speech sounds in English, and 3) mapping the speech sounds to the appropriate letter symbol (for more information on this, see Chapter 5). He reminds us that children will have the most difficulty with insights about speech sounds, or phonemic awareness. Children can learn to visually distinguish many different symbols and they can learn to say a particular sound when they see a symbol; however, if they do not understand that speech sounds are the building blocks for words, they will struggle.

In this chapter we have distinguished different "ph" terms because understanding this teacher jargon is important. We have provided a simple scope and sequence framework that reflects how children become aware of larger sound units and eventually smaller ones. We have also provided a collection of lively activities to suit preschoolers. Phonemic awareness does seem complicated, but it just cannot be skipped. Think of it as a vitamin for your alphabetic instruction.

References

Adams, M. J., Foorman, B. R., Lundberg, I., & Beeler, T. (1998). The elusive phoneme. *American Educator, 22*(1), 18–29.

Anthony, J. L., Lonigan, C. J., Burgess, S. R., Driscoll, K., Phillips, B. M., & Cantor, B. G. (2002). Structure of preschool phonological sensitivity: Overlapping sensitivity to rhyme, words, syllables, and phonemes. *Journal of Experimental Child Psychology, 82*(1), 65–92.

Castles, A., Rastle, K., & Nation, K. (2018). Ending the reading wars: Reading acquisition from novice to expert. *Psychological Science in the Public Interest, 19*, 5–51. doi:10.1177/1529100618772271

Cleary, B., & Darling, L. (1968). *Ramona the pest*. NY: Scholastic.

Ehri, L. C., Nunes, S. R., Willows, D. M., Schuster, B. V., Yaghoub-Zadeh, Z., & Shanahan, T. (2001). Phonemic awareness instruction helps children learn to read: Evidence from the National Reading Panel's meta-analysis. *Reading Research Quarterly, 36*(3), 250–287.

Juel, C. (1988). Learning to read and write: A longitudinal study of 54 children from first through fourth grades. *Journal of Educational Psychology, 80*(4), 437.

Kilpatrick, D. A. (2015). *Essentials of assessing, preventing, and overcoming reading difficulties*. John Wiley & Sons.

Liberman, I. Y., Shankweiler, D., Fischer, F. W., & Carter, B. (1974). Explicit syllable and phoneme segmentation in the young child. *Journal of Experimental Child Psychology, 18*(2), 201–212.

Lundberg, I., Frost, J., & Petersen, O. P. (1988). Effects of an extensive program for stimulating phonological awareness in preschool children. *Reading Research Quarterly*, 263–284.

Morais, J. (1991). Phonological awareness: A bridge between language and literacy. In *Phonological awareness in reading* (pp. 31–71). New York, NY: Springer.

Muter, V., Hulme, C., Snowling, M., & Taylor, S. (1997). Segmentation, not rhyming, predicts early progress in learning to read. *Journal of Experimental Child Psychology, 65*(3), 370–396.

National Reading Panel (US), National Institute of Child Health and Human Development (US). (2000). *Teaching children to read: An evidence-based assessment of the scientific research literature on reading and its implications for reading instruction: Reports of the subgroups.* National Institute of Child Health and Human Development, National Institutes of Health.

Roush, B. E. (2005). Drama rhymes: An instructional strategy. *The Reading Teacher, 58*(6), 584–587.

Suggate, S. P. (2016). A meta-analysis of the long-term effects of phonemic awareness, phonics, fluency, and reading comprehension interventions. *Journal of Learning Disabilities, 49*(1), 77–96.

Shaywitz, S. E. (2003). *Overcoming dyslexia: A new and complete science-based program for reading problems at any level.* Knopf.

Wagner, R. K., Torgesen, J. K., & Rashotte, C. A. (1994). Development of reading-related phonological processing abilities: New evidence of bidirectional causality from a latent variable longitudinal study. *Developmental Psychology, 30*(1), 73.

Willingham, D. T. (2017). *The reading mind: A cognitive approach to understanding how the mind reads.* NY: John Wiley & Sons.

4

Shared Reading and Interactive Writing to Teach Print Concepts and the Alphabetic Principle

In a recent opinion editorial for *Education Week*, Heidi Anne wrote about a pattern that she has seen with phonics instruction:

> To access phonics, children must have certain insights, or the system will make no sense.
>
> Students often learn letters but don't know, for example, that print runs left-to-right or that words are groups of letters separated by space—insights called print concepts. Similarly, students learn letter-names but do not understand the alphabetic principle—that symbols represent speech sounds ("cat" equals 3 symbols, 3 sounds). . . . We are putting the cart before the horse if we drill letter/sounds without also teaching print concepts and the alphabetic principle.

Children do not naturally learn how print works unless teachers, parents, or older siblings show them the way. Sometimes educators dive right into the most intricate parts of the early literacy equation, letter-sounds, without helping children understand how the system works, how the parts work together, or even the larger purposes of the system (meaning!). Alongside alphabet and phonological awareness instruction, we must back up, turn our scopes to a wide-angle setting, and teach children how print works. When we focus exclusively on letters without a parallel focus on how print works, we are teaching the parts absent of the whole. It's as if the children are working on this long, important project, but we are drilling different types of stitches, needles, and fabrics without telling them that the whole purpose is to weave a beautiful quilt.

What are "Concepts of Print?"

In the early 1990s, clinician M. M. Clay (1993), turned our attention to what she called concepts of print. From watching children very carefully, she observed that children often did not understand things about print that teachers and other adults assumed they did. She observed, for instance, that at the very early stages children often did not understand that print, the lines and circles on the page, actually told the story in a book and not the pictures.

"Well, it seems obvious," points out Vera, "but actually lots of kids do not even pay attention to the print. I mean the pictures are the most interesting to them. You have to draw their attention to the print." This is one of the earlier concepts, differentiating print, a symbolic system, from pictures, which are less abstract. There are other understandings about print, concepts we have grouped in Box 4.1, from the easiest to the most complex below.

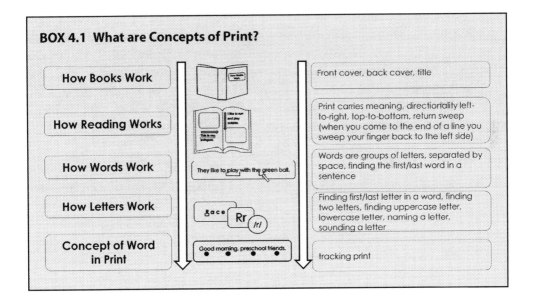

Concept of Word: The Most Critical Print Concept

"Well, they catch on pretty fast to simple things like print being the place to tell the story, but other things, like figuring out the difference between a letter and a word, takes time. And coordinating their finger with a line of text, that's the hardest, but it's fun to watch." explained Mei, a Head Start teacher in San Francisco.

Mei is correct; not all concepts of print are created equal. Usually, children can find the front and back cover, understand directionality, and differentiate pictures from print more easily than they can track words on a page. Eventually, as they spend more and more time participating in shared reading and writing, children narrow their focus to pinpoint where one word ends and the next begins. Their minds and insights are like a microscope that, at first, can only detect the fuzzy green boundaries of a leaf, but then focuses precisely to bring the cell walls and cytoplasm into focus. So, children at first notice that words are carrying meaning, and then they might notice that the words stay the same each time, that there is a connection between print and speech. Slowly they "see" that words are groups of letters separated by spaces, and they use beginning letter-sounds to coordinate print tracking.

Eventually, children show a very solid understanding of words in print; it comes into such clear focus. This occurs when a child can accurately point to words in a memorized line of print (Ehri & Sweet, 1991; Henderson, 1981; Morris, 1983; Morris et al., 2003; Smith, 2012). We call this "concept of word in print" or "fingerpoint reading." It's when children memorize a line and then use one-to-one matching to touch words and say them at the same time. This pointing and voicing requires coordination of a physical act (pointing), speaking, hearing, timing, and understanding spatial organization on the page. Although it may seem like "real reading," it is not.

Children go through three phases as concept of word in print solidifies, which are: 1) no concept of word in print/inaccurate pointing (Developing), 2) some concept of word in print—can point to some words but not multisyllabic words (Rudimentary), and 3) full concept of word in print—can point to all words (Firm) (Blackwell-Bullock et al., 2009; Morris, 1983; Morris et al., 2003). These phases are described below.

Full Concept of Word

In this example, the child is repeating a line from *Brown Bear, Brown Bear* (Martin & Carle, 1984), and pointing to the words. The top line of the table shows the words in the line, the next row shows the child's voice, and the check mark indicates that the child is pointing to a word. Here, the text, the child's voice, and the pointing all match up. In particular, the child knows that when she gets to the multisyllabic words like "yellow" and "looking," she must keep her finger on the same word. She knows that those two syllables for yellow only signify one word.

Text:	I	see	a	yellow	duck	looking	at	me
Child Reciting:	"I	see	a	yellow	duck	looking	at	me.
Child Pointing:	√	√	√	√	√	√	√	√

No Concept of Word/Little Pointing

In this illustration, there is little match between text, voice, and pointing. The child is trying to point to the words in the same line of text. As this example indicates, the child is saying the entire line of print but she is pointing to the word "see." She is saying, "I see a yellow duck looking at," and then she points to the last word "me" at the end. She knows the ending of the sentence, but she is not matching words and speech.

Text:	I	see	a	yellow	duck	looking	at	me
Child Reciting:		*I see a yellow duck looking at*						*me.*
Child Pointing:		√						√

In this other example, the child starts with I and then just runs her finger quickly under the print while saying all the words without pausing.

Text:	I	see	a	yellow	duck	looking	at	me
Child Reciting:	*I*	*see*	*a*	*yellow*	*duck*	*Looking*	*at*	*me.*
Child Pointing:	√						→	

Some Concept of Word

As a child is gaining control over voice, print, and pointing, he will show progress but struggle with multisyllabic words. In the example below, the child is doing well until he gets to the words "yellow" and "looking." Then he hears the multisyllabic word parts and moves his finger to the next word. So, on the second syllable of the word *yell-ow*, he points to *duck*.

This is not surprising, because syllables are very prominent in speech. They are big "chunks" of sound, and the child in this situation does not yet understand that words that are longer visually are often longer orally as well. When children have some level of phonological awareness of syllables, it helps them with finger pointing (Mesmer & Lake, 2010; Mesmer & Williams, 2015). However, the most useful information that children have to support accurate pointing is beginning sound knowledge.

Text:	I	see	a	yellow	duck	looking	at	me		
Child Reciting:	"I	see	a	yell	-ow	duck	look	ing	at	me
Child Pointing:	√	√	√	√	√	√	√	√	?	?

Concept of Word Is NOT "Teaching Preschoolers to Read"

We have both spent time with preschool teachers who get a little uncomfortable about print concepts, especially fingerpoint reading, print tracking, or other concept of word activities. "Teaching three-year-olds to read, it is just ridiculous," observed Juanita, an experienced Head Start teacher. We agree that for most children it is; however, there are precocious children who are able to begin learning to read because they have command of letter-sounds and they are phonologically aware. But teaching print concepts and concept of word is decidedly *not* "teaching children to read." When children track print or find letters, they are not decoding words or reading in a traditional sense. They are relying on context, memory, and other pre-and partial-alphabetic strategies as they name words (Ehri, 2005). Often, they would not be able to differentiate between similar words or read them in isolation. If you took *yellow* out of the *Brown Bear* sentence, they would not be able to read it. They also interchange similar looking words like *look* and *took* the same way.

Assessing Concepts of Print and Concept of Word

A Simple Assessment for Concepts of Print

Before being able to connect letters, sounds, and words, a child must be able to recognize the differences between letters, words, and other symbols as well as know how books "work." This brief assessment (Figure 4.1 in Appendix B its entirety.) should take about five minutes to conduct. The teacher presents images and asks the child to point to either a letter, number, picture, or word. In the second section, the child is presented with a mock book page and asked to identify pictures versus text and directionality (which way text is read).

Concept of Word in Print

Once a child shows some command of the idea of words and letters along with some letter-sound knowledge, it is possible to assess concept of word in print. This simple measure (Figure 4.2 in Appendix C in its entirety.) does not require children to memorize a rhyme or story. Instead, the teacher simply says a sentence and asks the child to repeat it. Then the teacher says the sentence, points to the print, and asks the child to do the same. The assessment takes about five minutes.

Shared Reading for Learning Print Concepts

We strongly suggest that preschool teachers use two well-supported practices, shared reading and interactive writing, to support concepts of print, concept

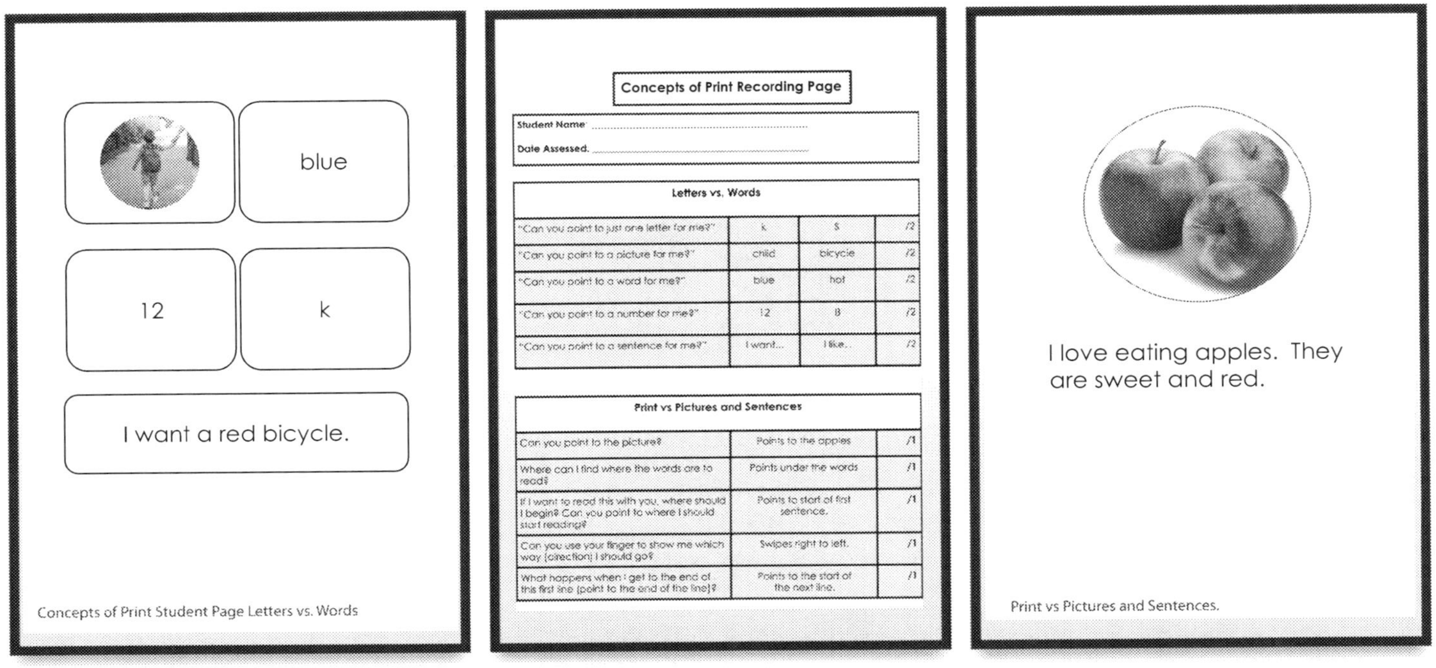

Shared Reading and Interactive Writing ◆ 67

Figure 4.1 Concepts of Print Assessment Preview (the assessment can be found in its entirety in Appendix B).

68 ◆ Shared Reading and Interactive Writing

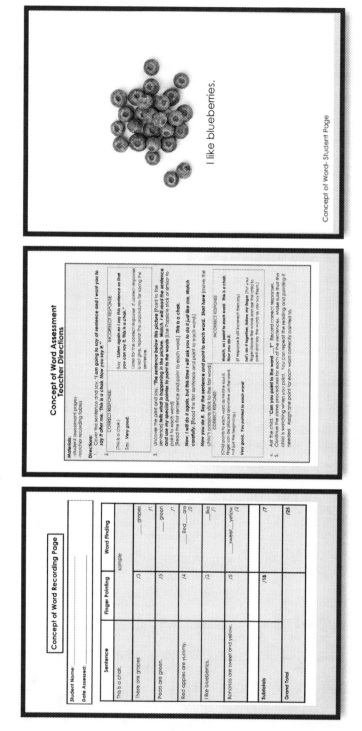

Figure 4.2 Concept of Word Assessment Preview (the assessment can be found in its entirety in Appendix C).

of word, and the alphabetic principle. Both of these teacher-guided practices demonstrate reading and expressive writing in a whole group setting following specific routines. They typically only take about ten minutes per day, but their effects accumulate powerfully across days, weeks, and months to pay off in developing children's insights about print.

We suggest that, on a daily basis, preschool teachers do either a shared reading or interactive writing session with their students. Other practices and techniques include working with environmental print, setting up literacy-rich centers, and eventually letting children fingerpoint "read" caption books at the more advanced stages.

What is a "Shared Reading?"

"Shared reading" is a specific type of read aloud, the purpose of which is modeling concepts of print for young learners. The teacher "shares" the reading responsibilities with the children as she models reading and pointing to print, saying the lines of print, finding words or letters, and moving the pointer across the lines. After modeling, children participate by finding words, showing where the print starts, finding important letters, identifying long words. To give children a good view of the print, the teacher uses a large book (1.5 x 3 feet) or digital projectable to read the book while pointing to the print and talking about other aspects of the book.

Without teachers calling their attention to print, children will only naturally look at words, letters, and sentences during a book reading less than 10% of the time (Ann Evans & St. Aubin, 2005). In one study, when teachers prompted children to think about the print, they focused on it over 20,000 more times than when there was no teacher instruction (Justice, Pullen, & Pence, 2008).

During a shared reading, the teacher will have a goal. The teacher might ask the children, "Where do I start my reading? Can someone come help me turn the page? Do I read here (the pictures) or here (the print)? How many words are there? Where do I go when I finish this line? Can you find a letter Cc on this page? Let's point to the words and say them together. How many words are on this page? Which word is longer?" (Justice et al., 2008; Zucker, Ward, & Justice, 2009; Nevo & Nusbaum, 2018).

Shared reading is not "teaching children how to read" but modeling the process and carefully asking them to "help" at different times based on what they need to understand. In practice, it may look like a traditional reading lesson to the non-expert, but it is most decidedly not. Children are memorizing lines of the book, but they are not really internalizing the spellings of words or retaining them in memory that way. They are not sounding out or decoding words, and they are not likely to recall the words outside of the book line. A shared reading shows young children, in a meaningful context, how to apply their emerging knowledge of literacy, alphabet, and print. It's showing a child, "Look at that Aa you learned, it is used to write words, that tell us ideas or make us laugh." Without a teacher demonstrating how to use letter knowledge, how words work, or how print operates, children are learning letters in a vacuum. Shared reading gives them the "big picture."

Shared reading is not grabbing a book off the shelf for read aloud to quiet children right before rest time. (Of course, that's not a bad thing to do, but it is not shared reading as we define it.)

> Shared reading is a specific type of instructional read aloud to model for children how print works. It is highly participatory; in fact, that's the very point—children participating!

We believe that the timing of a shared reading should be at the beginning of the day when attention is fresh, and children will more likely be ready to absorb the details of a shared reading. Read alouds that expand children's knowledge and vocabulary should also be a regular practice, but the shared reading, due to the types of texts that work best for it, is not usually that type of activity. Rich, extended texts with detailed stories, and non-repetitive, non-rhyming content typically characterize books read for knowledge building.

How to Do a Shared Reading

The hallmarks of "shared reading" are rereading the same text at least three times over several days to build familiarity with the words and sentences. Teachers often use texts or songs that are memorable with repeated sentences and/or rhymes (e.g., *"Not I," said the duck. "Not I," said the horse.; I went walking. What did I see? I saw a black cat looking at me.; Twinkle, twinkle, little star.*) See Box 4.2, below, a checklist for choosing books for shared reading. After reading the texts, once children are familiar, teachers invite them to "share" in reading the book, to help point to print, know where to start, find letters, and/or locate words. We suggest following a routine that we've compiled based on several studies (Blackwell-Bullock, Invernizzi, Drake, & Howell, 2009; Justice & Ezell 2004; Justice, Pullen, & Pence, 2008; Justice, Kaderavek, Fan, Sofka, & Hunt, 2009;. Zucker, Ward, & Justice, 2009; Nusbaum & Nevo, 2018).

BOX 4.2 Checklist for Choosing a Book for Shared Reading

- ❑ Is the print large enough?
- ❑ Is the book large enough to see from a distance? Or, if a projectable, can it be seen?
- ❑ Is the print consistently placed on the page?
- ❑ What font is used? Are the letters clear?
- ❑ Are the words and pictures clearly separate?
- ❑ How many sentences are on each page?
- ❑ Are the sentences too long?
- ❑ Are there multisyllabic sentences?
- ❑ Is the content memorable? Song? Poem? Predictable Story? Repetitive text?
- ❑ Is the content understandable?
- ❑ Is the content fun? Relatable?
- ❑ Would you want to read it over and over?

Follow a Routine

- ◆ **Day 1: Read the book and get to know it (no print concepts)**
  Day 1 has two goals: 1) enjoying the poem or story and understanding its meaning, and 2) learning the text by memory.
    - Step 1. First reading: Read the book and talk about the characters, the funny parts, the interesting parts, and any other pertinent features.
    - Step 2. Second reading: Reread to build memory. Ask the children to chorally read "Say it with me!" (everyone reads together).

  Note: On Day 1, there is no pointing to words or asking questions about the print.

- ◆ **Day 2: Reread the book with teacher pointing and child participation to target print concept**
  Day 2 has three parts: 1) rereading the book, with choral reading; 2) rereading with teacher pointing to print (children watch and whisper words); and 3) targeted print participation.
    - Step 1. First reading: Reread the text and invite choral reading. Ask children to "read along with me."
    - Step 2. Second reading with pointing: Read and point to the words with a pointer or finger. "Watch me read. Look at my

finger. You whisper the words as I go." The purpose of this second read is to model pointing and direct child attention to print. Many will not be able to sort out exactly the words that are being pointed to, but over time and with repetition, this will come into focus. Don't abandon ship. It's most important to make sure that children are watching the print.

- Step 3. Ask print concept questions: Revisit pages and ask children to participate with questions about the targeted print concept. "Who can come show me where I read the story? Do I read here (point to pictures)? Do I read here (point to white spaces)? Do I read here (point to words)? Can you come show me?" (The print concepts would differ based on the development of the student.) See Box 4.3 What to Say to Prompt Attention to Different Print Concepts.

♦ **Day 3/4: Reread with some child pointing and child participation to target print concept**

Note: The shared reading can extend to a fourth day if time permits, using the Day 3 routine.

- Step 1. First reading: Read and point to the words with a pointer or finger. Ask for child participation. "Watch my pointer. Say the words as I point." The teacher may purposefully vary the speed of the pointing to draw attention to the word being said, "My pointer is not working really well today. Sometimes it wants to go fast and sometimes it wants to go slow. Watch where it goes and say the word that it points to." Another technique is to quiet down on certain words or pause entirely to allow the children to "fill-in" words that are particularly easy. For example, "Twinkle, twinkle, little ____. How I wonder what you ____."

(Note. If you do use a rhyme that is also a song, we suggest *reading* the song during shared reading as opposed to singing. At times, the rhythm of a song can be a little fast and can blur words together. We like to tell children, "We are not going to sing this right now but we will read it slowly.")

- Step 2. Second reading with child pointing (if appropriate): If appropriate, ask a child to come up and point to the words as the group says them. With threes, and young fours, this might not be appropriate; instead, the teacher can use hand-over-hand to point to words or just ask the children to find the beginning of a sentence (See Boxes 4.4 and 4.5 for Examples of Shared Reading Pages).
- Step 3. Ask print concept questions: Follow Step 3 above (See Box 4.6 for Great Poems Songs and Stories for Shared Readings and 4.7 for A Warning about Nursery Rhymes).

BOX 4.3 What to Say and Do to Prompt Attention to Different Print Concepts

How Books Work

Cover
- The author gave this book a name (read title)
- What do you see on the front of this book?
- This is the name of the person who wrote this book. (point to author's name)
- This author wrote the book for his children. (dedication page)
- This is the front of the book.

How Reading Works

Direction
- Where on this page should I go if I want to start reading?
- Point to the words as you read
- Track the print to show directionality (left to right)
- This is the first page, this is where we start reading.

Print vs. Picture
- Look at the apple in the picture.
- This picture adds to what we just read.
- Do you see the bunny's brown fur? What color did you think they would be?
- The cat is talking, the words are all BIG to show us he is talking loud.

How Letters Work

- Can you find a letter?
- Can you find the letter ___?
- Circle known letters
- Counting letters in a word
- Using letters to start words
- Do you see a word that begins with the letter B?

How Words Work

- Counting or circling words
- Tracking words
- Point out frequently used words (I've seen the word "is" a lot in this book)
- Match words/labels to pictures (This is a picture of a cookie, the word cookie is written right here point at word)
- Long words vs. Short words (Listen to me say the word "elephant" and the word "red." Which one is long? Which is short?
- Where is the long word in the book? Where is the short word?
- Words are groups of letters, how many words do you see on the first page?
- Look! These words are the same.
- The bear is thinking...what do you think the words in his thought bubble say?

74 ◆ Shared Reading and Interactive Writing

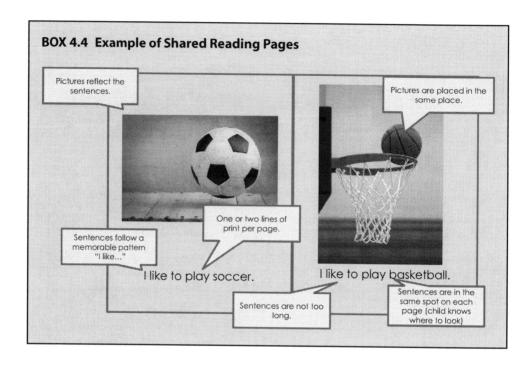

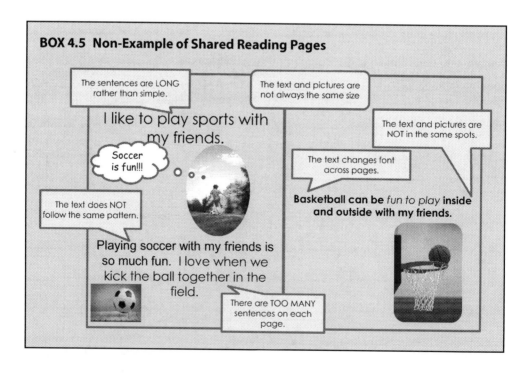

BOX 4.6 Great Poems, Songs, and Stories for Shared Reading

Poems/Songs:

Read-Aloud Rhymes for the Very Young selected by Jack Pretulsky
Hi, Koo!: A Year of Seasons by Jon Muth
The Neighborhood Mother Goose by Nina Crews
Little Poems for Tiny Ears by Lin Oliver
Digger, Dozer, Dumper by Hope Vestergaard

Stories:

Brown Bear, Brown Bear, What Do You See? by Eric Carle and Bill Martin Jr.
Pete the Cat: I Love My White Shoes by Eric Litwin; art by James Dean (and other Pete the Cat stories by James and Kimberly Dean)
It looked Like Spilt Milk by Charles Shaw
Where is the Green Sheep? by Mem Fox
Llama Llama stories, created by Anna Dewdney
Penguin series by Salina Yoon
A Big Mooncake for Little Star by Grace Lin

BOX 4.7 A Warning About Nursery Rhymes

A Warning About Nursery Rhymes

Nursery rhymes do serve as useful tools in teaching young children. Their rhythm and rhyme are also very appealing to children. Nursery rhymes use playful language, but that does not mean that they are all happy in nature and origin. We must be careful to look at nursery rhymes with a critical eye. Many nursery rhymes date back a hundred or more years and come from a variety of historical periods. These rhymes often contain themes of conflict, hardships, and unfortunately, racism. Many commonly known rhymes date back to the mid-1800s and early 1900s in the United States and have clear racist ties. Often the lyrics have now been changed, but it is important to note that they have a past linked to use in minstrel shows, racist lyrics that

> have sometimes been changed, and were written to depict hatred. Below is a list of some nursery rhymes and their questionable origins (Abad-Santos, 2014; Maiti & Naskar, 2017; Ulen, 2020).
>
> ★ Jimmy Crack Corn (1840s, performed in minstrel shows; original lyrics)
> ★ Eenie Meenie Miney Mo (early 1800s; original lyrics)
> ★ Five Little Monkeys/Ten Little Indians (originally published in the 1860s; later lyric changes and used in 1940s minstrel shows)
> ★ Oh! Susanna! (1840s; rhyme refers to a slave who is made out to be unintelligent)
> ★ The Icecream Song (Do your ears hang low) (published in the 1910s; original lyrics)

Shared Interactive Writing

What is Shared Interactive Writing?

The mirror image of shared reading is shared interactive writing. As with shared reading, shared interactive writing is a group lesson in which the teacher models writing and spelling through a briefly composed text that all children can see (See Table 4.1). The text might be written on a large chart paper propped up on an easel or may be projected digitally using a smartboard. Interactive writing starts with a meaningful message containing words and/or sentences that the children suggest. Collaborating with the group of children, the teacher guides them through various activities based on their knowledge, counting words, hearing sounds, and thinking about letters. The result is a message using conventional (accurate) spelling. The teacher will "share the pen or pointer," inviting young learners to write parts of words, find letters on an alphabet strip to use, or even write short two- and three-letter words on the shared classroom chart. The practice takes only ten minutes, and a chart can be completed in one day (if short) or be developed across several days (Roth & Guinee, 2011). Although a shared composed text is the final outcome, the *process* of composing, using foundational skills, and rereading messages is the most important part of interactive writing. Interactive writing lessons can be a useful place to model forming letters correctly, but it is not a time for detailed handwriting instruction.

Table 4.1 Examples of Teacher Language for Each Level of Interactive Writing

Instructional Goal	Language for Shared Reading	Language for Interactive Writing
Counting Words (Easiest)	"Let's count the words we want to write. I will put up a finger for each word. I will draw a line for each word. Let's say the words we want to write as I point to the lines."	"So our sentence is '*We like chocolate milk.*' Let's say it again and count. *We* (put 1st finger up), *like* (put 2nd finger up), *chocolate.* That's a long word, *chocolate*, but it is one word (put 3rd finger up), *milk* (put 4th finger up). Four words. *We like chocolate milk.* I will make a line for each word on our chart as a say it *We* (draw line), *like* (draw line), *chocolate* (draw line), *milk* (draw line)."
First Sounds (Harder)	"I want to find the word 'goat.' What sound do I hear at the beginning? /g/ What letter spells that sound /g/? Can you see it on the alphabet chart? Where is it? How do I write it? Yes! A circle and then a hook. All in one stroke."	"I want to write milk. What sound do I hear at the beginning of mmmmmilk? Say that with me mmmmmilk. What do you hear? How would I show that sound?"

(continued)

Table 4.1 Cont.

Instructional Goal	Language for Shared Reading	Language for Interactive Writing
All Sounds (Hardest) [Note: Many preschoolers will not get to this level.]	"Oh here's a short word. Can we read *it*? Let's say that sound iiiit. iiit. Oh I start with Ii then write Tt. I wrote 'it!'"	"*It is snowy*! Let's write that first word 'it.' What is the first sound /i/? What letter? That's right Ii. Can I ask Maddie to take my pen and write a capital Ii? Now let's say that whole word and listen for the second sound iiiii t. Oh, I hear /t/. How do I show that sound? Taylor, that's a letter you know. What is it? Yes! Tt. Can you come write a lowercase Tt after this?"

In preschool, the following goals, from easiest to hardest, are typical learning goals with Interactive Writing: a) identifying the number of words; b) hearing and writing first sounds in words; and c) hearing and writing all sounds in short, simple words with the CVC, VC, CV patterns. (Note: In grade 1 and beyond, interactive writing may have more complex instructional foci.) Below are examples of teacher language for each level of interactive writing.

How to Do an Interactive Writing Lesson

Figure 4.3 below shows the steps of a preschool interactive writing lesson. There are two phases, a Prewriting and Thinking phase, where the teacher and students discuss the content of the writing, name the sentence or words, and then repeat the message orally so that they can remember it, and a Writing phase, where the teacher models a portion of the message and then shares the pen with the students. The last step is reading what was written while pointing to the text.

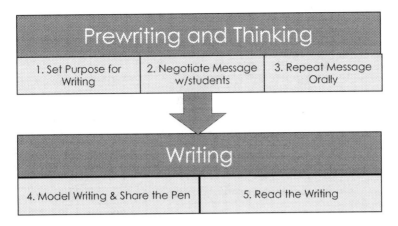

Figure 4.3 Interactive Writing Lesson.

Step 1: Purpose for Writing

In this step, the teacher presents the children with an authentic reason to write and begins a discussion. Some of the ideas, in Box 4.8, provide topics that might be based on sentences. Some topics require a week's worth of work to build sentences. Other ideas might be better suited to lists and labels. "You have to find something that they can get excited about and that is not too hard," explains Donna, a preschool teacher in Head Start. "One time, I started this one off about a recipe that was too long and the kids just lost interest. Also, I get so sick of the 'Morning Message.' You know, *Today is ___. We are going to ___. The weather is___.* It's not a bad idea here and there, but if that's interactive writing every other day, it's so boring."

After planning the purpose, the teacher leads a discussion. For example, "Do you remember yesterday when we went to Explore Park with that big playground? What did you like? Remember when we went to the firehouse? Can you share with me what you saw?"

Step 2: Negotiate Message

After discussion, the teacher states a sentence or a list of labels that will become the written message. Make sure to use words that the children supplied and, if the text will be a sentence, try to keep it short. I find that young children can remember about 5–6 words. Remember, you can add sentences and words to a strong topic on subsequent days. Here's an example: "So, Davon and Taylor talked about the fire pole and Maria talked about the lights and the siren. Hmmmmm, how about this sentence, 'We liked the lights and sirens.' Can we add the part about the fire pole on Wednesday? Davon and Taylor, help me remember the fire pole." (Note: Use Post-It notes to remember the children's ideas and come back to them. Interactive writing will be most successful when the messages are the children's.)

Step 3: Repeat the Sentence

This is a very basic but important step. Do not forget. In this step, the teacher simply restates the sentences and asks the students to do so at least two times. For example, "Our sentence is *We liked the lights and sirens*. Let's say that again. *We liked the lights and sirens*. Who can say it by themselves? Yes, let's all say it again together so we can remember it when we write it. *We liked the lights and sirens*." Memorizing the sentence sets up a scaffold for understanding how letters work in messaging. This, in part, is why it is very important to make sure that the children are supplying the ideas. They will remember their own ideas. If the children have not really internalized the sentence, the benefits of the lesson are not as strong.

Step 4: Modeling the Writing and Sharing the Pen

The next steps are when the teacher writes and invites the children to participate. At this point, the teacher must decide what she will give focus to and what she will not. With preschoolers, a teacher might not ask for help with every word. In certain situations, the teacher will simply write the word, describing it, and then move on. For example, "And this word is *the*, so I am writing *th* /th/ and *e*, which makes the /u/ sound." With other parts, the teacher will invite the students to help write. Based on the development of the children, we suggest teachers work on one of the three instructional goals stated above. For a lesson focusing on words, a teacher might say,

> Our sentence *We liked the lights and sirens* has a lot of words. Let's count. Okay, now I am going to put a line on the paper for each word and I am going to ask you to help me. [Teacher makes six lines.] Watch me point to each line as I say the sentence *We liked the lights and sirens* [Points to each line matching the word.] Who can tell me the first word? *We* Yes! Now I am going to ask someone to come up and show me where to write that first word—*We*. Which line would I use?

For a lesson focusing on the Ll letter-sound, the language might be like this,

> Alright, so I have put a line for each word in our sentence. Now I am writing the word *We* but I want your help for the next word. Listen to the first sound lllllliked. What sound do you hear? lllliked. What letter shows that sound? Yes, the letter Ll. Who can come up and write that letter Ll here? [point to second line.]

Next, the teacher would then write *the* without instruction and then solicit help with the word *lights.*

Step 5: Reread
In the last step, the teacher leads the children in rereading the sentence, pointing to the words and, if appropriate, asking individual children to come up and point.

BOX 4.8 Ideas for Authentic Weekly Interactive Writing Texts

Ideas for Authentic Weekly Interactive Writing Texts

Holiday Fun
Visiting the _____
Thank You
Book-based responses
    (e.g., Brown Bear; If You give a Kid a Cookie)
How-to texts
    (care for a plant; make muffins)
Weather
Diagrams with labels
    (winter clothes; setting the table; on my plate)
Fall is
    (Spring is; Winter is; Summer is)
Labeling a child mural
    (map of our classroom; animals)

A Few Cautions
In late kindergarten and first grade, interactive writing will often involve the teacher modeling the writing of each word in a sentence and each sound in every word. For example, a teacher might have the sentence *We love snow* and guide the children through finding the sounds in *we* and then writing the letters, and then finding the sounds in *snow*, and writing the letters. This is appropriate in late kindergarten/first grade because children have a certain fluency with letters. It is decidedly not appropriate (and, frankly, tortuous) in most preschool settings.

    In a preschool classroom, a teacher might select one word to work on but simply write the other words, or a teacher might decide to focus on the first sounds in two words with simple consonant sounds. So, in the case of *We like snow,* a teacher might say, "So I am writing the word *We,* and now I want your help with the first sound in *like,*" or, if the preschool group is working on counting words, she might say, "Listen, *We like snow,* let's say it *We like snow.* Let's count the words. Get your fingers ready. Say the first word '*We.*' Now put up a finger. Say the next word '*like,*' and put up another finger."

Other Techniques for Building Concepts of Print

Children's first interactions with print typically occur in a social setting. They begin to explore the print in their homes and communities, in addition to being read to. These early experiences are connected to application and context of the text. As you know, these early experiences set the stage for their later learning. As children enter formal school settings, their interactions with print often become removed from context and disconnected from the application or meaning print holds. We suggest the following to help build concepts of print by using these environmental print and play examples in your classroom.

Finding Environmental Print EVERYWHERE

Print can be found all around us. When we suggest finding environmental print, we mean more than reading signs. In addition to symbols or logos, environmental print includes words and letters (e.g., Paw Patrol). Learning to find letter cues in logos and pictures helps children focus on letters and become awarene of print concepts. Using environmental print has been shown to aid children in understanding what words and letters are, and that they hold meaning (Neuman, Hood, & Ford, 2013; Vera, 2011). Encouraging students to look at the signs around their town, school, and classroom can be beneficial. Add to these opportunities by creating environmental print for your classroom. This can be done by recreating signs, logos, or symbols that have letters or wordsand connecting them to your current themes or lessons. For example, if learning about foods and healthy eating, use images, empty boxes, and signs that you would find in a grocery store or at a farmers' market. The colorful signs may actually help children attend to the print, increasing their opportunities for learning about print (Neuman, Hood, & Ford, 2013). Also, encourage your school to set up opportunities to interact with print in the hallways, on the playground, or in the dismissal areas.

Building a Play Environment to Enhance Literacy Exploration

As a teacher of young children, you know the power of play. As we have said before, we strongly encourage the use of play to promote literacy activities.

What we love about this is that play is most likely already a part of your instruction. With a few changes, you can provide meaningful opportunities for literacy during play. If you don't already, label your classroom with words, and keep those labels at eye level for your students! When setting up play opportunities for your students, create clear spaces for specific types of play (e.g., kitchen play area). In your play areas, add materials that support literacy. You should consider three things in selecting these materials: are they appropriate, authentic, and useful (Neuman & Roskos, 1990). Appropriateness and utility are closely tied. Appropriate means the object is natural and safe for the child to use (e.g., keeping markers and crayons for office play, but saving scissors for when direct adult supervision is possible). Utility means that the object has a function that the child is familiar with (e.g., using a shopping bag to carry groceries in). An authentic material is one that would naturally be found in the child's environment. For example, in a post office, envelopes, boxes, labels, and stamps are authentic, while a magnetic board with letters would not be authentic in that setting. Literacy-enhanced play provides increased opportunities for interaction with text and also gives literacy a purpose. The play is not exchanged for literacy, instead "play becomes more purposeful" (Neuman & Roskos, 1990, p.218).

Fingerpoint "Reading" In Caption Books
Fingerpointing is a child's ability to track the print with their finger, pointing at each word as they "read." This might be a good activity for older four-year-olds who have a lot of letter-sound knowledge. This is best done using familiar text, such as a rhyme, that the child has memorized or a text with captions. A caption book is a simple book made with an image and a caption on each page. Caption books typically follow a pattern (See Figure 4.4.) and often use a sentence stem (I like …). Short sentences are important when developing this skill with young children.

Chapter Summary

Many times, we see preschool teachers overwhelmed with the requirements of teaching the alphabet, and we see children dazed and confused about the meaning of all the symbols flying at them. Although most teachers know about print concepts and the alphabetic principle, they do not have a set of ready practices that support teaching print concepts. What we see is an occasional mention at the beginning of a read aloud with a smaller book. These embedded "mentions" are not powerful enough or systematic enough to make a difference. We have shared these two research-based, high impact

Figure 4.4 Caption Book Example.

practices, shared reading and interactive writing, because they make a difference. Both should take place several times a week in preschool classrooms. Both advance children's broad conceptual understandings of what reading and writing are and why they are learning letters. Repeated modeling also helps them with the "big picture," the "next steps" in their literacy journey. So, do not cut this short in the race to do phonological awareness and alphabet instruction. These practices must reside side-by-side with explicit, systematic alphabetic instruction.

References

Abad-Santos, A. (2014, May 21). *What should we do with our racist folk songs?* Vox. www.vox.com/2014/5/21/5732258/the-racist-childrens-songs-you-might-not-have-known-were-racist

Ann Evans, M., & Saint-Aubin, J. (2005). What children are looking at during shared storybook reading: Evidence from eye movement monitoring. *Psychological Science, 16*(11), 913–920.

Blackwell-Bullock, R., Invernizzi, M., Drake, E. A., & Howell, J. L. (2009). Concept of word in text: An integral literacy skill. *Reading in Virginia, XXXI*, 30–36.

Clay, M. M. (1993). *An observation survey of early literacy achievement.* Heinemann, 361 Hanover St., Portsmouth, NH 03801-3912.

Ehri, L. C. (2005). Learning to read words: Theory, findings, and issues. *Scientific Studies of Reading, 9*(2), 167–188.

Ehri, L. C., & Sweet, J. (1991). Fingerpoint-reading of memorized text: What enables beginners to process the print? *Reading Research Quarterly, 26*(4), 442–462.

Henderson, B. B. (1981). Exploration by preschool children: Peer interaction and individual differences. *Merrill-Palmer Quarterly of Behavior and Development, 27*(3), 241–255.

Justice, L. M., Pullen, P. C., & Pence, K. (2008). Influence of verbal and nonverbal references to print on preschoolers' visual attention to print during storybook reading. *Developmental Psychology, 44*(3), 855

Justice, L. M., & Ezell, H. K. (2004). Print referencing. *Language, Speech, and Hearing Services in Schools.*

Justice, L. M., Kaderavek, J. N., Fan, X., Sofka, A., & Hunt, A. (2009). Accelerating preschoolers' early literacy development through classroom-based teacher–child storybook reading and explicit print referencing. *Language, Speech, and Hearing Services in Schools, 40*(1), 67–85.

Maiti, A., & Naskar, D. (2017). Of deception and dogma: The delusive history behind nursery rhymes. *European Journal of English Language and Literature Studies, 5*(4), 27–52.

Martin, B., & Carle, E. (1984). *Brown bear, brown bear*. Puffin books.

Mesmer, H. A. E., & Lake, K. (2010). The role of syllable awareness and syllable-controlled text in the development of finger-point reading. *Reading Psychology, 31*(2), 176–201.

Mesmer, H. A. E., & Williams, T. O. (2015). Examining the role of syllable awareness in a model of concept of word: Findings from preschoolers. *Reading Research Quarterly, 50*(4), 483–497.

Morris, D. (1983). Concept of word and phoneme awareness in the beginning reader. *Research in the Teaching of English, 17*(4), 359–373.

Morris, D., Bloodgood, J. W., Lomax, R. G., & Perney, J. (2003). Developmental steps in learning to read: A longitudinal study in kindergarten and first grade. *Reading Research Quarterly, 38*(3), 302–328.

Neuman, M. M., Hood, M. & Ford, R. M. (2013). Using environmental print to enhance emergent literacy and print motivation. *Reading and Writing, 26*, 771–79. https://doi.org/10.1007/s11145-012-9390-7

Neuman, S., & Roskos, K. (1990). Play, print, and purpose: Enriching play environments for literacy development. *The Reading Teacher, 44*(3), 214–221. Retrieved December 15, 2020, from www.jstor.org/stable/20200594

Nevo, E., & Vaknin-Nusbaum, V. (2018). Enhancing language and print-concept skills by using interactive storybook reading in kindergarten. *Journal of Early Childhood Literacy, 18*(4), 545–569.

Roth, K., & Guinee, K. (2011). Ten minutes a day: The impact of interactive writing instruction on first graders' independent writing. *Journal of Early Childhood Literacy, 11*(3), 331–361.

Smith, F. (2012). *Understanding reading: A psycholinguistic analysis of reading and learning to read.* Routledge.

Ulen, E. (2020, September 23). *8 children's nursery rhymes that are actually racist.* Reader's Digest. www.rd.com/list/childrens-nursery-rhymes-that-are-actually-racist/

Vera, D. (2011). Using popular culture print to increase emergent literacy skills in one high-poverty urban school district. *Journal of Early Childhood Literacy, 11*(3), 307–330. https://doi.org/10.1177/1468798411409297

Zucker, T. A., Ward, A. E., & Justice, L. M. (2009). Print referencing during read-alouds: A technique for increasing emergent readers' print knowledge. *The Reading Teacher, 63*(1), 62–72.

5

Teaching Letters and Letter-Sounds

Landon was a sweet boy that we encountered in a kindergarten classroom. With a gentle smile and brown hair, he always arrived at school dressed and ready-to-go. By the end of the day, he was satisfactorily a bit more ruffled, with a shirt untucked from doing the monkey bars, a dab of chocolate milk in the corner of his mouth from lunch, and a few stray marks on his hands from the magic markers he loved. Landon followed directions, got along with peers, nodded his head during lessons, and did what the teacher told him to do. In about February, his teacher, Kyle, talked to us about Landon and his letter knowledge:

> "We've been doing letters a lot. In fact, we work on a letter a week. We write the letter, talk about the sound, and complete these pages where they circle all the letters. You know like, if we're doing Cc, they circle all the Ccs. I mean he does those sheets right every time! He always circles the right ones. I just don't know why he hasn't learned more. But I'm not worried. He'll get it when he's ready."

The discussion with Kyle was revealing, and, as we watched, we could see that the instruction seemed always to be whizzing around Landon at breakneck speed. During whole group lessons he glanced around at his peers to "find answers" or chime in. At his desk, he was able to visually discriminate letters and circle target letters each week, but we could not tell if he knew any sounds. There was no

DOI: 10.4324/9781003130918-5

small group instruction, so it was difficult to know what he was really understanding.

Kyle and Landon are very typical of teachers and students that we see. Many adults are teaching letters and assuming that children like Landon are learning letters. They see nodding. They hear correct answers, and they assume that it is all working. And, like Kyle, many are not concerned when a student does not know many letters late in the year. With Landon, we did have concern. Whereas most kindergarteners in February know more than 10 letters, Landon knew only Aa, Bb, and Cc and then also Ll and Mm because these were the first letters in his first and last name. In addition, we were not even sure that Landon knew the most important information about letters, the letter-sounds or grapheme-phoneme correspondences (GPCs). With just a little connection between research and practice, we believe that letter instruction could be far more effective.

In this chapter, we cover alphabet instruction soup-to-nuts, beginning with a section about exactly what it means to "know letters." Often, teachers and parents do not think about the many different aspects of letter knowledge that children are expected to know, and breaking this down is important. Then, in the next section we provide some basic information about teaching letters. Many teachers, like Kyle, are using antiquated approaches that should be replaced. With just a little bit of knowledge about what we know about letters and sounds, alphabet instruction can become more effective. In the third section we highlight several "best practices," things that teachers should do as they teach the alphabet. Finally, in the last three sections, we offer a scope and sequence, assessment, and a collection of activities.

What Does it Mean to "Know Letters?" The Alphabetic Principle and Beyond

Parents say it all the time: "Well, she knows all her letters!" To the professional educator, this statement can be hard to interpret. Does this mean that the child knows *about* letters? Does the parent mean the child can recite the letters orally? Does this mean that the child points out a letter or two in signs? Does this mean the child can name the letters? Does this mean that the child can say letter-sounds?

When we say that children "know their letters," we are not talking about one thing. Actually, there are many different parts of letters that children must learn, from naming letters to knowing letter-sounds to using them and writing them.

Naming letters

When we say, "naming letters," we mean that a child can look at the letter and tell us the label for both the upper- and lowercase forms. For example, "This one (Bb) is called 'bee,' and this one, Cc, is called 'see.'" We know from research that when children can name the letters, they are likely to become successful readers later down the line (Adams, 1990).

We teach letter-names in the US because letter-names do help, in some cases, with learning the letter-sounds, but they are not typically taught in the UK or in other programs. Sometimes teachers get carried away with naming the letters; however, knowing the names of the letters is not enough to become a good reader. You must know letter-sounds and then how to decode and spell words using those, and then you must have background and knowledge and vocabulary in order to understand what you read. Basically, knowing letter-names is necessary but not sufficient, and, honestly, it is not the most important piece of letter knowledge (Lonigan & Shanahan, 2009; Invernizzi & Buckrop, 2018).

Letter-sounds

When we say that children know their letter-sounds, we mean that they can identify the common sounds when they see the single consonants and vowels (see Chapter 2 for a listing of the common letter-sounds (GPCs) taught in the emergent years). Children demonstrate letter-sound knowledge when they can say the sound /s/ when they see the letter Ss, for instance. As we described in Chapter 2, we typically teach single consonant sounds, long vowel sounds, and short vowel sounds. In order to eventually read, children must know letter-sounds. Some preschool teachers forget this, and interviews with them show that the letter-sounds did not get as much attention as letter-names (Gerde, 2019). Whenever we are teaching a letter, we teach *both* the name *and* the sound *always*, even if only letter awareness is the goal (see Box 5.1: Letter Awareness: Should I Teach Both Letter-Names and Letter-Sounds?)

Box 5.1 Letter Awareness: Should I Teach Both Letter-Names and Letter-Sounds?

The *Head Start Early Learning Outcomes* identify Letter "Awareness" as a goal for young preschoolers, ages 3–4. The standard reads:

Shows an awareness of alphabet letters, such as singing the ABC song, recognizing letters from one's name, or naming some letters that are encountered often.

> Even though the goal at this stage is simply to name and recognize some letters, it is best practice to always present both the letter name and letter sound. For example, "This is the letter Dd. It is how we write the sound /d/ like in David."
>
> If we do not provide the letter-sound information, which is the information used to read words, then we are shortchanging children. In fact, in the UK and in Montessori classrooms, letter-names are not taught, only sounds. Some children will pick up and retain letter-sounds easily, just as some children will be able to repeat a musical tune more easily, skip earlier, or understand spatial relationships. Further, by sharing the letter-sounds, we are helping children extract the letter-sound information that is in some letter-names like Bb, Dd, Jj, Kk, Pp. Make it a habit: letter-names + letter-sounds.

Writing letter forms

In order to decode, children need to know the letter-sounds in a word, but, in order to spell, they must be able to write the letters. Children need to be able to form the letters efficiently and accurately as soon as they can, and this requires focused instruction in handwriting. Now, for young preschoolers, aged 36–48 months, fine motor activities will often be constrained to cutting, drawing, sculpting, and some "pretend" writing. From three to four years old, children can practice making markings that will eventually be used in writing letters. Three-to-four-year-olds can copy straight lines (both horizontal and vertical) and curved lines (Cheyney-Collante, Gonsalves, Duggins, & Bader, 2020). Children at this age can trace larger letters on cards, trace letters, "air write" letters, and make letter writing attempts on very large paper. Darla, a teacher in a faith-based preschool program, shares, "We have so much fun making letter shapes with sand, finger paint, pudding, and shaving cream. And it does really pay off. One little guy said to me, 'Yeah. That's Gg, I made that hook on it in the sand tray.'" After 48 months, handwriting instruction can begin in earnest, where children learn how to properly make letters. At this age, children should be able to copy necessary marks for letter formation (Cheyney-Collante et al., 2020).

Using letters: The alphabetic principle

Sometimes teachers, parents, and even children think that if they can sing the alphabet song then they have what they need, but, as discussed in Chapter 2, all the letter naming in the world makes no difference if children do not understand the alphabetic principle.

Teaching Letters and Letter-Sounds ◆ 91

Not knowing the alphabetic principle, is like having a shiny new toy but no batteries to go with it; it doesn't work. Like a cool new toy without batteries, a child who knows their letters and letter-sounds without having knowledge of the alphabetic principle has no power. The toy can do little without the batteries. The outside of the toy may be shiny and interesting, but the toy doesn't serve its purpose. Knowing letters and letter-sounds creates a nice exterior perception, but hides the fact that the child has no idea of what those letters and sounds can do!

Figure 5.1 Alphabetic Principle Metaphor.

Simply put, the alphabetic principle is that visual symbols represent individual speech sounds. It is the notion that letters form graphemes that represent speech sounds. It is the understanding that writing is a visual representation of speaking, a parallel mirror image of sorts.

Without this understanding, children really will not go far. Yes, they can memorize letter-names and even sounds, but they will not be able to use the information (see Figure 5.1). They must understand the organization of letters and sounds in English. As described in Chapter 4, as they are teaching the alphabet in targeted lessons, teachers illustrate the alphabetic principle through sharing big books and projectables with children as they show children how letters, words, and sentences work. In terms of letters, there are three essential pieces of information we typically teach, including letter-names, letter-sounds, and how to write the letters.

What You Should Know Before Teaching Letters

When we work with preschool teachers, we can often feel the tension in the air around teaching letters. In recent years, there has been a huge shift towards emphasizing emergent literacy. Many preschool teachers have just been thrown into this new content. Stella, a 30-year veteran, explains, "It's like one year it's all about play and then, Bam! All of a sudden, it's like 'teach letters, teach letters, teach letters.' So we are teaching letters." We can sympathize. For many, there has been little training and little acknowledgment of the fact that working with three-year-olds is very different than working with kindergarteners. There are three clarifications that we believe are very important to make about letters. These include the role of visual discrimination, or being able to tell one letter from another, the order in which children typically learn letter information, and the pivotal role of phonemic awareness in making letter-sound knowledge "stick."

Visually Discriminating and Naming Letters is Only a First Step

As mentioned at the end of Chapter 3, children need three abilities to use letter-sounds (Willingham, 2017). First, they need to be able to tell one letter from the other, visually, to see what makes one letter different from another. This requires analyzing the visual features: the lines, circles, and positions of these. This means knowing that what distinguishes an uppercase Ff and Ee, for example, is the single line at the bottom, or seeing that the difference between a lowercase Ff and Tt is the top (and sometimes a bottom) "hook" (see Figure 5.2, below). Second, children need to have the insight or understanding that words are composed of speech sounds or phonemes, as we discuss in Chapter 2. In order to make sense of "letter-sounds," they must shave off that first sound of a word. Third, children need to map or connect the correct speech sound(s) to the correct visual letter symbol; they must know letter-sounds.

Of the three skills, children learn some are easier than others. "They know their letters. We've got that done." explained Nina, a Head Start teacher. "Look, at these cool games!" I watched as she showed me letter "candy canes," where children matched letters. This indicated that they could visually match the forms and attend to the features, and this was a great first step, *but* only a first step. In fact, of the three parts described, visual discrimination is actually the easiest (Willingham, 2017). Beyond visual discrimination, children must learn names, attach specific speech sounds to the letters, and then,

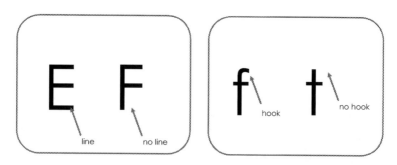

Figure 5.2 Visual Discrimination of Letters.

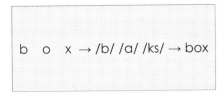

Figure 5.3 Children a) discriminate visual letter forms; b) attach sounds to each letter form; then c) sound out words.

eventually, use that information as they synthesize visual symbols into whole words (see Figure 5.3). The eventual goal of letter instruction is quick identification of the major sounds for consonants and the short and long sounds for vowels. That's what children need to decode a word—rapid use of the visual forms to cue the speech sounds. Thus, simply matching two similar visual forms or uppercase and lowercase forms is not enough, and it's not even the hardest part. Once the visual forms are sorted, letter-names and letter-sounds must be taught. We have this funny way of thinking about it. We like to say you could tap a child on the back in the middle of a candy store, show him a letter, and he could automatically tell you the sound in the middle of all of the distraction. It eventually needs to be that automatic if it *is to be used.*

The Typical Sequence in Which Children Learn Letters

It will come as no surprise to an observant preschool teacher what researchers have established about the order in which children typically learn letter-names. Most children in the US learn letter-names first and then letter-sounds. If you are working with a child who knows some of their letter-names, the letters are usually Aa, Bb, Cc, Xx, and Oo, as well as any letter at the beginning of the child's name (Drouin, Horner, & Sondergeld, 2012; Justice et al., 2009; Piasta, Petscher, & Justice, 2012).

"I know the sound of [Ww] said Wilson," a bright little four-year-old from Georgia. "Duh." Again, this would not be a surprise to a preschool teacher. In fact, Wilson is harnessing his knowledge of the letter name to help him with the sound, and, though it does not work with Ww, it does work with some letters (see Box 5.2). When children know some letter-names *and they have some level of beginning phonemic awareness,* they tend to learn the sounds of letters with the sound in the first part of the name (Bb /b/) (Evans et al., 2006; McBride-Chang, 1999; Huang, Tortorelli, & Invernizzi, 2014; Jones & Reutzel, 2012; Share, 2004). Then, they learn letter-sounds where the target sound is at the end of the letter name ("Eff, El"), and, finally, they learn those tough ones like Ww, Hh, Xx.

BOX 5.2 Order of Letter Learning

Order of Letter Learning

Uppercase letter name
- Salient forms (e.g. letters in own name)

Lowercase letter name
- With similar uppercase "parents" (e.g. Cc, Oo, Ss)
- With dissimilar uppercase "parents" (e.g. Aa, Bb, Gg)

Easiest letter-sounds (GPCs)
- With names that have the target sound at the beginning of the letter name (Bb, Dd, Jj, Kk, Pp, Tt, Vv, Zz)

Easy letter-sounds (GPCS)
- With names that have the target sound at the end of the letter name (Ff, Ll, Mm, Nn, Rr, Ss)

Hardest letter-sounds (GPCs)
- With no information in the name (Hh, Yy, Ww, Xx)

Phonemic Awareness is the Key to Making Letter-Sounds "Stick"

As we discussed in Chapter 3, language play to build phonemic awareness is key to making the information stick. With letter-sounds, the key phonemic awareness skill is being able identify the initial sound in a word. When a child has that insight, then he will more easily learn and retain letter-sounds than if he did not. In fact, a researcher found that many children can use letter-names to help them "figure out" the letter-sounds, but only if they already had some level of phonemic awareness. In other words, if children could orally identify the first sounds in *ffff*ish, *fffff*un, and *fffff*an, then they could use the letter name Ff to learn the letter-sound /f/. Phonemic awareness leads to the ability to infer sounds from letter-names. So phonemic awareness is key. It must accompany letter instruction on a daily basis.

Best Practices in Alphabet Instruction for Preschoolers

Because letter knowledge is so obvious to adults, we find that people often just jump right in, but there is so much solid research and information about how to do it right. Teaching the alphabet the right way is deceptively harder than it seems, and, for this reason, we offer eight best practices to guide instruction. These best practices sections are "power packed" translations of many research studies that will ensure efficient and effective instruction. Specifically, these practices include:

- Be systematic and explicit
- Teach letters in isolation but model use in shared reading and writing
- No more "Letter of the Week"
- Choose letters to teach purposefully
- Cycle through letters over time
- Use short, brisk, predictable lessons
- Use multisensory techniques
- Clip your sounds for stop consonants

Be Systematic and Explicit

When teachers hear the terms "systematic and explicit," they sometimes get a little panicky. One preschool teacher said, "So that's like worksheets? Little kids' in rows with number 2 pencils? Right?" What it really means is that you have a plan, an order to teach letters, and use direct language in teaching (Piasta & Wagner, 2010; Stahl, 2015; Lonigan & Shanahan, 2009). Specifically, systematic refers to the teaching plan and explicit refers to the teaching language. Systematic simply means that teachers follow a guide to letter teaching that lists the letters to be taught and the order in which to teach them. This is a scope and sequence, and it is the essential "systemic" part of the equation. We like to think of it as a recipe, one that can be "doctored" with extra spices or ingredients, but one that ensures that your work results in learning. This does not mean that teachers do not take advantage of beautiful teachable moments (e.g., "Oh yes. Look there is a Bb on that 'Boys' sign.").

> However, the driver of alphabet instruction is a scope and sequence and not simply the serendipitous timing of the letters that may (or may not) come up in the classroom or a shared reading.

Explicit means how you teach on a daily basis or how you talk to children about the sounds represented by letters. This means that the teacher is direct with children about letters. For example, a teacher would say, "This letter, Ll, has the sound /lll/ (pointing to the letter as she is saying the sound)." A less explicit teacher might say something like this, "Look. Lllllemon, lllllllollipop, and lllake. Can you hear that? /llll/?" This language is a nice first step, but the teacher never directly tells the children that a particular letter symbol represents a sound.

Teach Letters in Isolation but Model Use in Shared Reading and Writing

Teachers sometimes get confused about letter instruction. Of course, for children to really learn the shapes of letters, their uppercase partners, and their sounds, they must study them individually. How else would you be able to devote time to the analytical processes required? This does not mean that teachers do not point out, discuss, find, or write letters within meaningful contexts like stories, charts, or shared big books. As we note in Chapter 4, shared reading and interactive writing must be a weekly occurrence in classrooms. Preschool teacher Barbara explained, "Isolation or context? Well both. They can't focus without isolated examples, but they need to know why they are learning letters." We agree; when teaching a focused lesson on a particular letter, that letter must be promoted in isolation.

No More "Letter of the Week"

Many teachers like to use a "Letter of the Week" approach because it is tidy, can be used to drive fun thematic units, and seems like it provides children with the necessary time to learn a new letter. More recently, however, teachers are moving away from this. Jenelle explained, "It was fun to do an apple unit in September and other stuff, but it started to feel like the tail wagging the dog, like the units were the reason for what I was doing and not the letters themselves." Jennelle hits on one of the reasons that this approach is not useful—all letters do not need the same amount of time. As explained, some letters are easier than others, and often children already know certain letters (Aa, Bb, Cc, Xx, Oo) and so they will not require the same amounts of time.

We note four problems with the letter of the week (see Figure 5.4, below). First, teachers move on regardless of mastery. It is all about a tidy organizational structure and not learning. Second, as mentioned, all letters are not equally difficult. Some letters will need more review (e.g., H, W); others will already be known (e.g., A, B, C, X) and will not need repetition or much teaching. Third, letter of the week is not based on assessment or group needs—it is one size fits all with the change of a week serving as the instructional pivot point. Fourth, the letter of the week approach is too slow. With 26 letters and 36 weeks of instruction, almost two thirds of the school year is over by the time the entire alphabet is even introduced. All in all, letter of the week is something that more and more educators are abandoning (Jones & Reutzel, 2012; Piasta, 2014; Stahl, 2015; Sunde, Furnes, & Lundetræ, 2020).

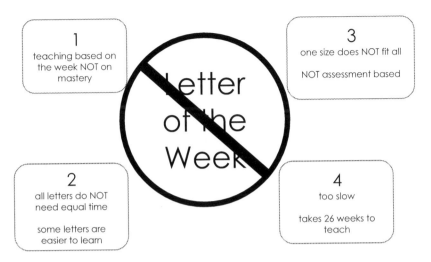

Figure 5.4 Four Problems with Letter of the Week.

Choose Letters Purposefully

Instead of choosing letters based on the alphabetic order over the course of 36 instructional weeks, you can use three approaches (Jones & Reutzel, 2012). (Just an aside; we have not been able to find conclusive research pointing to a specific order that is more effective than others.) As this little section will illustrate, there are multiple considerations including whether names or sounds are the focus, or whether visual contrasts versus sound contrasts are considered. We share this information so that teachers can be mindful of these as they plan (See Figure 5.5).

First, and very beneficial with preschoolers, is what is call the "Own-name advantage." Teach children their very first letters based on their own name and the names of their friends. Children's own names are among the first words that they learn, and the letters in their name can be an excellent source of first teaching. Usually children will learn the first letter in their name through this approach (Treiman & Broderick, 1998). In the activities section, we provide a four-week sequence of using names to help children learn to visually discriminate letters, learn names and sounds, and even some phonemic awareness. Learning letters based on names can be an excellent approach to the beginning of the year when children are getting to know each other (Cunningham, 1988). (Note: Using children's names is best at the early "Awareness Stage" because not all children's names match the most typical sounds that we teach. For example, *Juan* could be confusing, because we typically teach the /j/ sound for the letter Jj.)

With young children, teachers might also pay attention to the consonant sounds that speech and language specialists tell us are learned earlier (Justice et al., 2006). Usually, children can say the sounds for vowels very early and then the consonant sounds for n, m, p, h, t, k, y, f, ng, b, d, g, w, and s (Sander, 1972). Most children acquire harder sounds, such as l, r, v, z, sh, ch, j, zh, and th, after age four (Prather, Hedrick, & Kern, 1975). Thus, if you are teaching the sounds for these, children may be able to hear them but not correctly articulate them.

As any good Wheel of Fortune contestant will tell you, some letters show up in words more than others. Another approach to choosing letters is the frequency of a letter. Learning the more "popular" letters first is helpful. Here is a list from the most frequent to the least frequent consonants: Rr, Tt, Nn, Ss, Ll, Cc, Dd, Pp, Mm, Bb, Ff, Vv, Gg, Hh, Kk, Ww, Xx, Zz, Jj, Qq, Yy (Jones & Reutzel, 2012_.

We are sure that many preschool teachers looked at the list of frequently occurring letters and noticed several challenges. For example, if a teacher followed this list, then Dd, Pp, and Bb would be taught in very close sequence, and that's a problem because children often confuse these letters. Many teachers prefer to space those out and then review and clarify towards the end of alphabet instruction. Thus, at the beginning of instruction, children are likely to learn letters that are visually distinct more quickly.

Experienced teachers might also notice that the frequency list presents other challenges in terms of letter-sounds. When teaching letter-sounds, certain sounds are very similar. For example, the sounds typically represented by Ff and Vv are made in the same way (manner) and place in the mouth. The only difference is that /f/ is unvoiced, the vocal cords do not "buzz," and

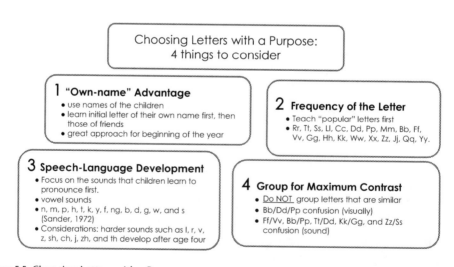

Figure 5.5 Choosing Letters with a Purpose.
(Cunningham, 1998, Jones & Reutzel, 2012, Justice, et al. 2006, Prather, Hedrick, & Kern, 1975, Treiman & Broderick, 1998)

/v/ is voiced, meaning the vocal cords *do* buzz. Thus, teaching these in close proximity is also not a good idea. (Note: The following pairs are also similar b-p, t-d, k-g, z-s).

Cycle Through More Than One Letter Per Week and Review

Several pieces of research suggest that teaching more than one letter per week is preferable (Jones & Reutzel, 2012; Roberts, Vadasy, & Sanders, 2018; Sunde et al., 2020; Vadasy & Sanders, 2020). In many of the studies, teachers introduced letters in brisk, simple lessons at the rate of one per day, or several per week. In general, this approach did not harm students, and, in fact, they often learned more letters under these conditions. In a study of kindergarteners, teachers presented letters two-at-a-time, and this was effective as well. One research team taught in "cycles," introducing letters and then cycling back to give more review and practice to those not yet mastered (Jones & Reutzel, 2012). Figure 5.6 shows easier and harder letter names and sounds.

Teach Short, Brisk, Predictable Lessons in Small Groups

With preschoolers, less is more. Darren explains: "Yep, short and sweet. Keep it focused, keep it fun and active, keep the routines the same, and when you don't have their attention, stop." Fortunately, young children make it clear to their teachers when they are not paying attention. We cannot emphasize enough how impactful small group lessons are with preschoolers (Piasta, 2014). In fact, small groups are actually more effective than one-on-one tutoring perhaps because the interaction amongst children supports learning (Piasta & Wagner, 2010). When children are in small groups, teachers can

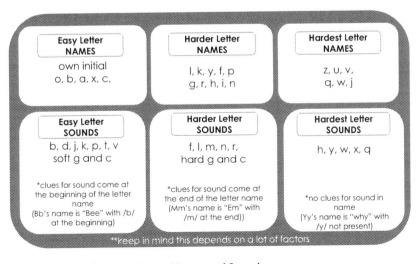

Figure 5.6 Easy, Harder, and Hardest Letter-Names and Sounds.

respond to them, make eye-contact, manage manipulatives, and give them feedback. We believe that small group instruction is the place for introducing new information and making sure that *each* child is getting it. As we described with Landon, at the beginning of this chapter, there was no small group instruction. Large group instruction is the place for review, large kinesthetic motions, songs, demonstrating the use of letters. Typically, a daily, 10–12 minute, focused small group lesson works (Jones & Reutzel, 2012; Piasta, 2014; Roberts et al., 2018; Roberts & Sadler, 2019). Every letter lesson should begin with a simple phonemic awareness activity (beginning sounds) that frontloads the specific letter-sound (GPC) being taught. (For beginning sound awareness instruction, see the Initial Sounds Activities at the end of Chapter 3.) In a letter lesson, the teacher would start with oral work on the target sound. For example, she might say, "We are going to be learning the way to spell the sound of /t/. Let's play a game, Tommy Tiger likes things that start with /t/. He likes ttttttuna. He likes ttttarts. He likes tttturtles. Let's go around the circle. You can even be silly. Tommy Tiger likes taters!"

After just a few minutes of beginning sound work, several activities may follow. In several studies teachers conducted very simple games with preschoolers to practice letters (Roberts, et al., 2018; Roberts, 2019). One game, called "Animal Game" asked children to "feed" the animal the new letter. In "Feed the Alligator," for example, children would "feed" the alligator Aa's. In another activity, Little Letter Books, children would practice naming letters in small books with pages.

Use Multisensory Techniques

Whenever we involve children fully, using all of their senses, we see positive outcomes. Orton–Gillingham is a specific approach to teaching that uses seeing letters and the way the mouth moves when making sounds, hearing sounds, writing letters, and feeling the shapes of letters (Ritchey & Goeke, 2006). In this approach, and the many associated derivations, children pay attention to the way sounds feel in the mouth and look when pronounced. They trace letters, air write, and even tap sounds in words as they are learning phonemes. Some teachers use mirrors to show children how to make sounds (e.g., "Look when I say /m/ my lips are pressed together. When I make /b/ I press my letters and then 'pop' the sound."). Below are several techniques to help children learn the sounds and shapes of letters:

- Air writing letters
- "Sand writing," where children write the letters in sand trays

- Tracing letters in large, grooved sand-covered tracks (like puzzle frames)
- Manipulating magnetic letters

In a recent study, one researcher (Neuman, 2018) had three-year-olds identify, trace, and write letters and words in environmental print (e.g., signs, labels on products, household items). The possibilities are endless when it comes to involving children. Just make sure that the activity accurately supports the goal—learning letter shapes and sounds.

Clip your Sounds on Stops: Avoid "Guh, Puh, Duh, Buh."

Author Heidi Anne recently reviewed some materials for an educational entrepreneur. The materials were really beautiful, with bright pages, clear letter forms, and helpful, direct instructions to teachers. But they had one very big flaw. For the stop sounds for Bb, Cc, Dd, Gg, Kk, Pp, Tt, the directions to teachers had this extra sound on the end. For Bb, the writer had written, "Say the sound "buh." Actually, this shows two sounds, /b/ and /ə/. When we teach these stop consonants, we want to try, as much as possible, to clip that /ə/ sound that comes right after the stop consonants. It is impossible to not have just a little bit of that whenever you say a stop sound (Willingham, 2017), but you can minimize it.

Assessment for Alphabet Instruction

What's the Goal in Preschool? How Many Letter-Names and Letter-Sounds?

Many preschool teachers are not exactly sure about the learning goals for letters with young children. How many letters is enough? With young children, we know that they should learn some letters and sounds, but exactly how many, and when, is less clear. At a minimum, children entering kindergarten, after completing pre-kindergarten, should be able to name at least ten letters, including either uppercase or lowercase forms. Some researchers, and the recent Early Learning Outcomes Framework, suggest that naming 18 uppercase and 15 lowercase letters may be a better benchmark (Piasta, Petscher, & Justice, 2012). About 65% of entering kindergartners know all of their letters (West, Denton, & Reaney, 2000), but only about 21% of children coming from Head Start into kindergarten know all letters (Diamond, Gerde, & Powell, 2008). The Head Start Early Learning Outcomes Framework

(ELOF) and Common Core State Standards in the English Language Arts (CCSS-ELA) provide some guidance (and we add some of our own) (National Governors Association Center for Best Practices, Council of Chief State School Officers; 2010

- 36–48 months (3–4 yrs)   Awareness of Common, Meaningful Letters (ELOF)
  - "Shows awareness of alphabet letters, such as singing the ABC song, recognizing letters from one's name, or naming some letters that are encountered often."
- 48–60 months (4–5 yrs)   Naming Half Letters and Knowing Some Sounds (ELOF)
  - "Recognizes and names at least half of the letters in the alphabet, including letters in own name (first name and last name) as well as letters encountered often in the environment."
  - "Produces the sound of many recognized letters."
- By 60 months (5 yrs)   18 Uppercase and 15 Lowercase Names with Many Sounds (ELOF)
  - "Names 18 uppercase and 15 lowercase letters."
  - "Knows the sounds associated with several letters." (We believe that this should say "many" letter-sounds and not several. In fact, the standard for 4–5 yrs does say "many.")
- 61+ months (kindergarten)   Mastery: Fluent and Automatic Letter-Sounds (CCSS-ELA)
  - "Recognize and name all upper- and lowercase letters of the alphabet."
  - "Producing the primary sound or many of the most frequent sounds for each consonant."
  - "Associate the long and short sounds with common spellings (graphemes) for the five major vowels."

Thus, from the perspective of standards, what we ask of children depends on how old they are, with three-to-four-year-olds becoming aware of letters, naming salient and common letters, with four-to-five-year-olds learning at least half of the letter-names and producing sounds for many of these letters, and the goal at five years, kindergarten entry, being naming 18 uppercase and 15 lowercase letters and some sounds. Thus, the focus in kindergarten would be to solidify all letter-names and letter-sounds along with writing letters. Usually, this is solidified by mid-kindergarten (University of Oregon Center on Teaching and Learning, n.d.; Invernizzi et al., 2004).

Our perspective is that the goal for preschool should be naming at least ten letters, with the hope that many children will learn more.

Assess Names First, Then Sounds

In line with the standards and expectations for preschool age children, our suggestion for assessment of letter-names and sounds is to assess names first. Since children typically recognize uppercase letter-names before lowercase letter-names, we suggest starting your assessment with uppercase letters and then moving forward with the lowercase letters. We suggest not assessing letter-sounds until students have acquired around 15 letter-names, and, typically, letter sound assessment is not attempted until around age four. The order that letter-sounds are typically developed differs from the order that letter-names are acquired; our assessment reflects this.

Scope and Sequence for Alphabet Instruction

Below, we have provided a scope and sequence to guide alphabet instruction in preschools for three- and four-year-olds. Each unit should take about three weeks and has a particular content focus and a set of "can-dos" for children. Units 1–8, about 24 weeks, focus on letter awareness, as described in the Head Start Early Learning Frameworks (Head Start ECLKC, 2020), and would be best for three-year-olds. The focus in these units is learning letter-names and their own names. (Note: Even though letter-names are the goal, both letter-names and letter-sounds are always taught.) Some of the later units in this group would also be useful for younger four-year-olds. The second half of the scope and sequence, Units 9–15, is for older children and focuses on letter-sounds correspondences. At this point, the focus becomes not only naming the letters but also learning the sounds that are represented by the letters. These units are most definitely best for four-year-olds. Note the structure of the letters scope and sequence and the structure of the phonological awareness scope and sequence are similar.

Activities for Alphabet Instruction

Early alphabet learning will focus on naming letters, recognizing letters in context (including their names), and matching upper- and lowercase forms. Letter-names and sounds should always be taught together, but activities for later letter learning will heavily emphasize letter-sounds and writing letters correctly.

104 ◆ Teaching Letters and Letter-Sounds

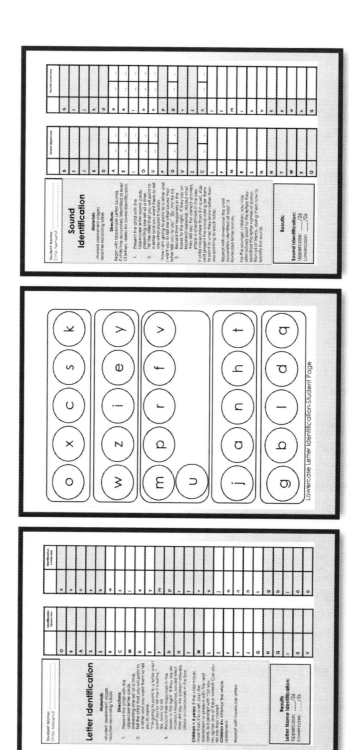

Figure 5.7 Letter Name and Sound Assessment Preview (assessment provided in its entirety in Appendix D).

Teaching Letters and Letter-Sounds ◆ 105

Table 5.1 Scope and Sequence for Alphabet Instruction

	Unit #/New Skill (three weeks/unit)	Teacher says …	Child can …	Skills to Review
Young three-year-olds	**1. Own Name (Recognizing)** Becoming aware of letters through own name.	Everyone has a name that we can write. Let's look at yours. This says "David." That's your name. The first letter is Dd. Look at all these names on the board. Can you find yours and move it to the right place?	Find name amongst a group. Name the first letter in his/her name.	
	Units 2–6 focus on introducing letters. The goal is for students to *name* some letters. However, always present *both* the name and sound and do some light initial sound phonemic awareness before working with letters.			
	2. Very Common Letter Names (A, B, C) Name the first three letters of the alphabet. Listen for the letter-sounds.[1] Initial Sound Phonemic awareness for /a/, /b/, and /k/.[2]	Let's use the alphabet chart to point to letters and sing the song. Watch my pointer. What is the first letter in the alphabet? Aa. It spells the sound /a/. Aaapple.	Name the uppercase and lowercase letters Aa, Bb, and Cc. Find words in the environment with these letters.	Find my name. Say the first letter in my name.

(continued)

Table 5.1 Cont.

	Unit #/New Skill (three weeks/unit)	Teacher says …	Child can …	Skills to Review
Young three-year-olds		PA: Let's play a game, Alan likes apples, ants, and Alice.	(Optional) Say the sounds for Aa, Bb, Cc.	
	3. Oo, Tt, Ss, Xx, Ll Letter Names Name these letters. Listen for letter-sounds. Phonemic awareness (initial sound)	(Same for Units 3–6) Let's use the alphabet chart to point to letters and sing the song. Watch my pointer. Let's find Tt like our friend TTTad. Can you find another Tt? PA: What do you think Tad likes? (toys, tables, Texas)	(Same for Units 3–6) Name the uppercase and lowercase letters. Find words in the environment with these letters. (Optional) Say the sounds for target letters.	Aa, Bb, Cc Letter Names
	4. Ee, Dd, Vv, Rr, Mm Letter Names (See above)			Oo, Tt, Ss, Xx, Ll Letter Names
	5. Ff, Jj, Kk, Ww, Yy Letter Names (See above)			Ee, Dd, Vv, Rr, Mm Letter Names

Teaching Letters and Letter-Sounds ◆ 107

Younger four-year-olds	Older three-year-olds	6. Gg, Hh, Ii, Nn, Pp, Uu (See above)		Ff, Jj, Kk, Ww, Yy Letter Names
		7. Review All Letter Names		
		8. Own Name (All Letters + Writing)	Your name David starts with a D. Can you name other letters in your name?	Name two or more letters in name.
		Names two or more letters in name.	I can show you how to write a capital D. It's a line and a half circle. You try.	Write, as appropriate, one or more letter in name.
		Writing attempts for letters in name.	Let's cut your name into two parts (D-avid). Put it together. Let's try three parts (D-a-vid).	Put 1–2 letters of name in order if cut apart.
		Begins to learn order of letters in name.		
		Units 9–15 focus on more advanced letter skills. The goal is for the children to name both upper- and lowercase letters and to learn letter *sounds*.		

(continued)

108 ◆ Teaching Letters and Letter-Sounds

Table 5.1 Cont.

		Unit #/New Skill (three weeks/unit)	Teacher says …	Child can …	Skills to Review
Younger four-year-olds	Older three-year-olds	9. Aa, Bb, Tt, Gg, Kk Letter Sounds Name the letter for both upper- and lowercase forms. Say the sound matching the letter. (Both short and long sounds for vowels.) Initial sound phonemic awareness.	Let's look at these pictures, paint, soap, pot, sack, peach. Which ones start with /p/? Paint? Let's find letters on our alphabet chart. I say a letter and you find it. (Pp). Point to the Pp. Let's say the sound that Pp spells /p/.	Say the sound associated with the letter (including short and long vowel sounds). Begin to properly make the written forms. Identify objects or oral words that start with the target sound.	
		10. Ii, Pp, Ff, Vv Letter Sounds (See above)	I want to write the word *purple*. How would I start that? Which letter would I use?		Aa, Bb, Tt, Gg, Kk Letter Sounds

Older four-year-olds	11. Uu, Jj, Cc, Zz Letter Sounds (See above)	Ii, Pp, Ff, Kk, Vv Letter Sounds
	12. Ee, Ss, Dd, Mm Letter Sounds (See above)	Uu, Jj, Cc, Pp, Zz, Letter Sounds
	13. Oo, Nn, Rr, Hh, Ll Letter Sounds (See above)	Ee, Ss, Dd, Mm Letter Sounds
Older four-year-olds	14. Ww, Xx, Yy, Qq Letter Sounds (See above)	Oo, Nn, Rr, Hh, Ll Letter Sounds
	15. Review all Letter Sounds	

1 Note. Always present *both* names and sounds, even though letter names are the goal early on.
2 Always present some light phonemic awareness *prior to* showing children letters and letter-sounds. This builds their awareness of speech sounds. See Chapter 3 Activities for Initial Sounds.

Awareness and Some Names: Exposure and Introduction

Learning my Name. Typically, children learn their names in three steps: recognition, building, and writing. In other words, they are first able to identify their name written on labels. Next, they recognize the individual letters that make up their names and can start to put them together (using magnetic letters, etc.). Finally, children begin to trace and write their names. Depending on the age of the children in your class, the writing portion may or may not be appropriate. Here we take these stages and suggest a four-week sequence of using names to learn the alphabetic principle.

Week 1. Students will learn to recognize their name as a whole, focusing on the first letter. As you start the year, you probably will have many things labeled already. We suggest that you pair the name labels with pictures of the students during this first week, so they are able to associate their names with their picture, and those of their classmates. In Anna's son's preschool room, he quickly learned "M" meant Matthew's space and "P" was for his best friend. We also suggest that you distinguish the first letter of each child's name by making it a different color or by underlining it. Visually, this makes the child look for that first letter (See Figure 5.8). Keep in mind, however, that, by mid-year, you would want to remove this cue.

Week 2. Students will look closer at the individual letters in their name, beginning to listen to the sounds each letter makes within their name. We suggest having students use manipulatives to break apart their names into individual letters. Using foam letters or letter cards to take apart their names allows them to recognize that their names are made up of individual letters (See Figures 5.9 and 5.10). This helps with the differentiation between letters and words as well as beginning to look at letter-sounds. Children can search through letters to find the ones they see in their name. This second week, we focus on identifying letters but not the order.

Week 3. Students will use manipulatives to build their name, allowing them to focus on individual letters and their sounds (blending into their names). Children will be encouraged to think about the order of the letters in their name. Focus on the letters that make up the first and final sounds in their name, as they are the easiest to hear. Activities that support this include building names with magnetic letters (provide only the ones they need to

Marie

Figure 5.8 Visually Distinct First Letter (Marie).

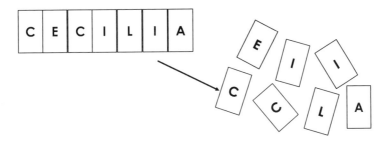

Figure 5.9 Breaking Apart the Letters in a Name (Cecilia).

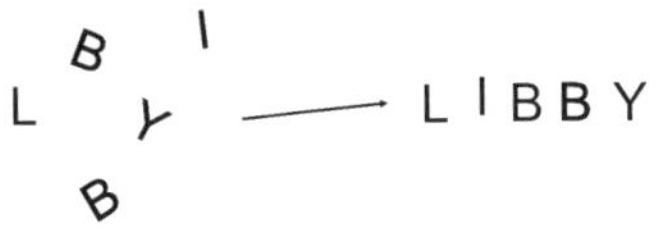

Figure 5.10 Building with Manipulatives (Libby).

build their names), or name puzzles, where they receive the letters in their names in mixed up order and put them together to build their name.

Week 4. Students will trace or write the letters in their names. Younger preschoolers will focus on writing initial letters only, while older preschoolers will attempt to trace and write their whole name. This week, we suggest you focus on initial sounds in the child's name and have them begin tracing and/or writing their initial letter using salt trays, paint, or large chart paper (see more activities below).

Below you will find activities to support visual discrimination and naming (weeks 1–3) and writing letters (week 4).

Environmental Print in My Community

Letter Hunt. Provide the children with a letter (or a few letters) to be searching for as you take a walk in your community. This is a great activity to encourage parents to try with their children, as it requires little to no supplies. Early learners may benefit from having a card with their letter(s) on it to help them remember what letter they are searching for and what it looks like. With caregivers, this activity can easily be done looking at road signs in the car, in the grocery store, or walking through a neighborhood.

Literacy Everywhere. Find areas of your school building or community that typically are not places you see literacy and infuse them with opportunities to practice letter identification, reading, etc. Do your kids line up in the hallway after lunch? Have letters taped to the wall that they can point to and identify. Do your students have to walk in a straight line in the hallways? Tape letters to the floor that they can identify as they step. Do students wait in a common area for pickup by bus or car? Have alphabet books available for them to flip through or magnetic letters to "play with" as they wait.

Visual Discrimination and Naming

Gone Fishing. This one may be best for warmer weather when you can break out the water table in the outdoors. Fill up your water table and add foam letters. We suggest only including the ones that your students have learned rather than all 26 at first. Children use fishing poles (you can make your own with wooden dowels, string, and a paperclip, or similar materials) to catch a letter. They must say the letter name before "releasing" it to be caught again.

Digging Around. Fill up your sand table or sensory bin with sand, kinetic sand, rice, or beans, and add plastic letters (or magnetic or foam). Have students use shovels, excavators, and other tools to dig up the letters. Like in the previous activity, we suggest starting with familiar letters.

Dough Play. Using dough, have students roll or squash it into a circle that they can then stamp letters into. This is best done with plastic letters like the ones you'd place on your refrigerator.

Color by Letter. These take a bit of preparation but are easy and fun for your kids who like to color or paint. Sketch out a simple picture (or find one online) and write letters to represent different colors. For example, the petals of a flower may be labeled Mm and the leaves Nn (Figure 5.11). Provide a key for students to follow. Keep the number of letters/colors simple (less than five on a picture).

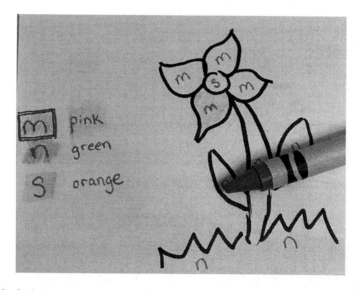

Figure 5.11 Color by Letter.

Advanced Letter Learning: Closing in on Letter-Sounds Writing Letters

Start Big. Provide spaces where students can make big motions as they begin to write letters. Encourage students to form letters or the marks needed to make letters such as curved lines/circles, straight lines (formed in different directions), and diagonal lines. Sidewalk chalk can be used outside on the pavement or inside on large pieces of black paper. Indoors, you can use a dry erase marker to allow children to draw on glass windows, glass doors, or even mirrors. Children love the opportunity to draw on something they usually aren't allowed to! Children also enjoy having large pieces of paper taped to the wall to allow them to make big lines with markers, paint, crayons, etc.

Sand and Salt. You won't need a lot of sand or salt for students to be able to do this activity. This allows children to trace letters or write letters without typical writing utensils. A small tray or box will need about 1–2 cm deep of sand or salt to be successful. Children can be prompted to draw lines, letters, or to trace a letter card you place under the sand or salt. Scented salt was a big hit at Anna's house. To make this, you add 2–3 drops of extract (lemon, mint, vanilla) and ½ teaspoon of vinegar to 1 cup of salt, shake it all together in a bag or cup, and let it air dry before using. Children can use their fingers, the eraser end of a pencil, or paint brushes to make letters.

Air Writing. This is a great whole group activity. As you write on an easel or whiteboard, the children "air write" the letters. This can be done with letters, names, or, later on in development, whole words. It allows the children to make the motions big and without worrying about messing up, since no-one can tell if they do!

Applying Letter Knowledge: The Essential Shared Reading and Writing Connection

As we detail in Chapter 4, *Shared Reading and Interactive Writing*, letter instruction should be occurring alongside purposeful alphabet instruction. During an interactive writing lesson, say the letter-names out loud while writing them, making sure to be using clear letter formations. While forming the letters, narrate for the children what you are doing: "Up, down, up, down makes an M." This allows them to take this narration with them as they begin to write on their own. Note similarities to other letters, "Ooops, I forgot to put the tail on my a, so it looked like an o."

For shared reading, incorporate alphabet books. They provide ample opportunities to identify letters and words that begin with those letter-sounds. After reading, allow students to access the books on their own by placing them in a reading center or in your classroom library.

As you read, display portions of the text and identify letters in the text. Focus on ones you are working on learning and those that have been mastered; it is often best to identify letters that come first in a word with younger learners. As you read, you should stop and circle letters in the text: "Do you see this letter? It looks like a tall line with another line sitting on top! We call this letter T!" You may also have children identify letters by giving each child a card with a letter on it and having them come up and find a letter in the shared text that matches it.

Make connections to student names as you read and write. For example, if writing the word "love," repeat the word and note to the children, "love begins with Ll. Llllll sounds like the beginning of Leila's name Llllll-eila."

Great Alphabet Books for Teaching Letter-Sounds

We encourage the use of alphabet books and know how there are thousands you can choose from. It is important to preview alphabet books to see what words are chosen to represent letters, because authors sometimes make a stretch when matching a word in order to fit the theme of the book. For example, Anna's children were given a book that used "Knuckle-boom loader" for the Kk page. While it fit the construction theme and had an awesome picture to accompany it, the Kn doesn't represent the /k/ sound, making it not the best for teaching that particular letter. Below, we provide a short list of some of our favorite alphabet books to help you get started on identifying books that might work in your classroom.

Chicka Chicka Boom Boom by Bill Martin, Jr. and John Archambault: What ABC book list is complete without this classic? The letters all climb up the coconut tree, then BOOM BOOM, they all fall down. This classic provides great letter examples, with Lois Ehlert's colorful but clean illustrations, but not too many opportunities to hear the sound of the letter. As the story goes, they get "turned around" when they fall from the tree, leading to the letters being presented in the second half of the book upside down, altered ("black-eyed p"), or sideways. For children that have developed a solid understanding of the visual shapes of letters, this is a good one! Children can even look at the mixed-up letters and try to identify them.

Letter Town by Darren Farrell: This book follows Bus Driver B as they drive throughout Letter Town picking up different letters along the way. The storyline is engaging, and the illustrations allow for children to seek and find letters that take on different personas (e.g., Baker B, Baby B, and Biker B all appear on the page for Bb). While the illustrations are colorful, the letters are not always crisp examples and may be confusing for a child without a developed understanding of the visual shapes of letters. For those ready to explore letter-sounds, however, this is a great choice!

Miss Bindergarten Gets Ready for Kindergarten by Joseph Slate: Miss Bindergarten and her 26 new students prepare for kindergarten in this book. It uses student names to lead the reader through the alphabet and uses a rhyming pattern as well. The author uses a different color to set apart the highlighted letter for each student, which helps distinguish it from the rest of the text. While the letter choices are clear, the text is often on a curved line. This one is good for introducing how letters are used in student names, as well as with older preschoolers who are listening for letter-sounds and preparing to transition to kindergarten themselves.

A Is for All the Things You Are: A Joyful ABC Book by Anna Forgerson Hindley: This book has beautiful, diverse illustrations and bold versions of the letters at the top of each page. The main text is simple (e.g., H is for Happy), but each page also includes a longer statement that connects to the word as well as a guiding question to make self-connections. The simple text would be perfect for younger students and could be added to with older preschoolers. The author uses simple examples that use the typical letter-sounds for each letter.

Apple Pie ABC by Allison Murray: This book follows a girl and her dog on a journey to make and enjoy an apple pie. Each page displays the uppercase letter in a large font, and most examples use the traditional letter sound. They do use eXit as the word example for Xx. This provides clear examples of the uppercase letters for children learning to identify letters, an adorable storyline, and, overall, good letter-sound examples.

LMNO Peas by Keith Baker: Travel through the alphabet with the beautiful illustrations of Keith Baker. Each page features a large uppercase letter surrounded by pictures and labels of occupations that begin with that letter. This book is great for children beginning to identify uppercase letters as well as those who are learning letter-sounds. The letters are crisp and clear, and the story ends with the question, "Who are you?" which could prompt a great letter art project for your students.

Summary

We know that alphabet instruction is one of the most important areas of preschool literacy. Children do need to learn letters and letter-sounds, and, as this chapter indicates, there is a great deal of information out there. Specifically, the research tells us how children learn letters, ways to choose letters to teach, as well as the letters that are easier/harder. High quality practices underscore the importance of engagement, phonemic awareness, short, brisk lessons, and multisensory techniques. As we described earlier, in Chapter 4, shared reading and interactive writing must also take place in parallel with focused alphabet instruction. Without this essential complement, children will not know what to do with their letter learning. Armed with ready-to-use information, this chapter can and will improve your instruction and help you to avoid some of the missteps that occur. No more boring drill. No more ineffective practices.

References

Adams, M. J. (1990). *Beginning to read: Thinking and learning about print.* Cambridge: MIT Press.

Cheyney-Collante, K., Gonsalves, V., Duggins, S., & Bader, J. (2020). A misunderstood fundamental: Developmentally appropriate strategies for letter formation in preschool. *Dimensions of Early Childhood, 48*(2)

Cunningham, P. (1988). Names: A natural for early reading and writing. *Reading Horizons, 28*(2), 25–30.

Diamond, K. E., Gerde, H. K., & Powell, D. R. (2008). Development in early literacy skills during the pre-kindergarten year in Head Start: Relations between growth in children's writing and understanding of letters. *Early Childhood Research Quarterly, 23*(4), 467–478.

Drouin, M., Horner, S. L., & Sondergeld, T. A. (2012). Alphabet knowledge in preschool: A Rasch model analysis. *Early Childhood Research Quarterly, 27*(3), 543–554.

Evans, M. A., Bell, M., Shaw, D., Moretti, S., & Page, J. (2006). Letter names, letter sounds and phonological awareness: An examination of kindergarten children across letters and of letters across children. *Reading and Writing, 19*(9), 959–989.

Gerde, H. K. (2019). Current practices for teaching letter and letter sound knowledge in preschool including strategies for improving instruction in these areas. *National Head Start Association Dialog, 22*, 76–83.

Huang, F. L., Tortorelli, L. S., & Invernizzi, M. A. (2014). An investigation of factors associated with letter-sound knowledge at kindergarten entry. *Early Childhood Research Quarterly, 29*(2), 182–192.

Invernizzi, M., & Buckrop, J. (2018). Reconceptualizing alphabet learning and instruction. In A. S. Dagen & R. M. Bean (Eds.), *Pivotal research in early literacy: Foundational studies and current practices*, 85–97.

Invernizzi, M., Sullivan, A., Meier, J., & Swank, L. (2004). *Phonological awareness literacy screening preK (PALS-PreK).* University of Virginia.

Jones, C. D., & Reutzel, D. R. (2012). Enhanced alphabet knowledge instruction: Exploring a change of frequency, focus, and distributed cycles of review. *Reading Psychology, 33*(5), 448–464.

Justice, L. M., Kaderavek, J. N., Fan, X., Sofka, A., & Hunt, A. (2009). Accelerating preschoolers' early literacy development through classroom-based teacher–child storybook reading and explicit print referencing. *Language, Speech, and Hearing Services in Schools*, 40(1), 67–85.

Justice, L. M., K. Pence, R. B. Bowles, and A. Wiggins. 2006. "An investigation of four hypotheses concerning the order by which 4-year-old children learn the alphabet letters." *Early Childhood Research Quarterly*, 21, 374–89.

Lonigan, C. J., & Shanahan, T. (2009). Developing early literacy: Report of the National Early Literacy Panel. Executive summary. A scientific synthesis of early literacy development and implications for intervention. *National Institute for Literacy*.

McBride-Chang, C. (1999). The ABCs of the ABCs: The development of letter-name and letter-sound knowledge. *Merrill–Palmer Quarterly, (1982-)*, 285–308.

National Governors Association Center for Best Practices, Council of Chief State School Officers. (2010). *Common Core State Standards in the English Language Arts*.

Neuman, M. M. (2018). The effects of a parent–child environmental print program on emergent literacy. *Journal of Early Childhood Research*, 16(4), 337–348.

Head Start ECLKC. (2020, November 1). *Head Start early learning outcomes framework: Ages birth to five*. https://eclkc.ohs.acf.hhs.gov/school-readiness/article/head-start-early-learning-outcomes-framework

Piasta, S. B. (2014). Moving to assessment-guided differentiated instruction to support young children's alphabet knowledge. *The Reading Teacher*, 68(3), 202–211.

Piasta, S. B., Petscher, Y., & Justice, L. M. (2012). How many letters should preschoolers in public programs know? The diagnostic efficiency of various preschool letter-naming benchmarks for predicting first-grade literacy achievement. *Journal of Educational Psychology*, 104(4), 945.

Piasta, S. B., & Wagner, R. K. (2010). Developing early literacy skills: A meta-analysis of alphabet learning and instruction. *Reading Research Quarterly*, 45(1), 8–38.

Prather, E. M., Hedrick, D. L., & Kern, C. A. (1975). Articulation development in children aged two to four years. *Journal of Speech and Hearing Disorders*, 40(2), 179–191.

Ritchey, K. D., & Goeke, J. L. (2006). Orton–Gillingham and Orton–Gillingham-based reading instruction: A review of the literature. *The Journal of Special Education*, 40(3), 171–183.

Roberts, T. A., & Sadler, C. D. (2019). Letter sound characters and imaginary narratives: Can they enhance motivation and letter sound learning? *Early Childhood Research Quarterly*, 46, 97–111.

Roberts, T. A., Vadasy, P. F., & Sanders, E. A. (2018). Preschoolers' alphabet learning: Letter name and sound instruction, cognitive processes, and English proficiency. *Early Childhood Research Quarterly, 44*, 257–274.

Sander, E. K. (1972). When are speech sounds learned? *Journal of Speech and Hearing Disorders, 37*(1), 55–63.

Share, D. L. (2004). Knowing letter names and learning letter sounds: A causal connection. *Journal of Experimental Child Psychology, 88*(3), 213–233.

Stahl, K. A. D. (2015). Using professional learning communities to bolster comprehension instruction. *The Reading Teacher, 68*(5), 327–333.

Sunde, K., Furnes, B., & Lundetræ, K. (2020). Does introducing the letters faster boost the development of children's letter knowledge, word reading and spelling in the first year of school? *Scientific Studies of Reading, 24*(2), 141–158.

Treiman, R., & Broderick, V. (1998). What's in a name: Children's knowledge about the letters in their own names. *Journal of Experimental Child Psychology, 70*(2), 97–116.

University of Oregon Center on Teaching and Learning. (n.d.). Official DIBELS Home Page: UO DIBELS Data System. https://dibels.uoregon.edu/

Vadasy, P. F., & Sanders, E. A. (2020). Introducing grapheme-phoneme correspondences (GPCs): Exploring rate and complexity in phonics instruction for kindergarteners with limited literacy skills. *Reading and Writing, 34*, 1–30.

West, J., Denton, K., & Reaney, L. M. (2000). *The kindergarten year: Findings from the early childhood longitudinal study, kindergarten class of 1998–99*. Washington DC: National Center for Education Statistics.

Willingham, D. T. (2017). *The reading mind: A cognitive approach to understanding how the mind reads*. John Wiley & Sons.

Appendix A

Phonological Awareness Assessment Teacher Directions

Materials:
- Teacher direction pages
- Teacher recording tables
- Optional: counting chips or other small manipulative

Directions:
Directions for each subtest are on the following pages.
Begin with the rhyme assessment and move on to the sounds Part I and II assessments.
If a student reaches frustration (0/4 correct), stop assessment.

Results:
A score of 8/8 (4/4 in an individual section) suggests the child has a good understanding of the concept. A score of 0–2 (out of 8) or 0–1 (out of 4) suggests that the child has minimal knowledge and is perhaps not ready for instruction in that area yet. A score of 3–6 (out of 8) or 2–3 (out of 4) suggests that the child is beginning to understand the concept but requires further instruction in that area.

Note: Concept of word should also be assessed as a part of phonological awareness; see separate assessment for this.

	Rhymes
Recognition	Model for the child, "Words that share the same ending sound, rhyme. *Dog, frog, hog,* and *jog* all rhyme. Let's rhyme together. I will tell you two words and you tell me if they rhyme. *Sit, fit*" If the child answers correctly, say "Good, let's try some more." If the child gives an incorrect answer, help by providing the correct response and restate what a rhyme is. "Let's do some more. I will tell you two words, and you tell me if they rhyme." Read the below sets of words. Record the child's responses (check if correct). <table><tr><td>1. jet – pet</td><td>3. car - cat</td><td></td></tr><tr><td>2. red – ran</td><td>4. bug - hug</td><td></td></tr></table>
Production	"Now you get to make up the rhyming word. I will tell you a word and you will tell me a word that rhymes. It can be a real word or a made up one! "Let's try one together. *Pig, fig (pause) lig, dig, mig.* It's okay to say silly, made-up words. "Now you try. I'll say a word, and you tell me a word that rhymes. *Dog*" (pause for the child to respond). If the child responds correctly, say "Good. Let's make some more rhymes." If they respond incorrectly, provide the correct response and restate the task. "Let's make some more rhymes. I will tell you a word, and you tell me a word that rhymes with it." Read the below set of words. Record the child's responses. <table><tr><td>1. bag</td><td>3. dad</td><td></td></tr><tr><td>2. rub</td><td>4. nut</td><td></td></tr></table>

	Sounds Part I		
Initial Sounds	"I am going to read a few words. We are listening for the first sound in the words. If I say *moon*, you will tell me /m/ because the first sound in *moon* is mmmm." *Make sure the child knows to tell you the sound and not the letter name.* "Let's try one. What sound do you hear at the start of *big*?" /b/ If the child provides an incorrect response, assist them by using the language in the first prompt. If the child provides the correct response, continue. "Now let's try some more." Read the below sets of words. Record the child's responses.		
	1. hat - hill	3. money - map	
	2. dog - duck	4. look - line	
Ending Sounds	"I am going to read a few words. This time, we are listening for the last sound in the words. If I say *sun*, you will tell me /n/ because the sound at the end of *sun* is nnnn." *Make sure the child knows to tell you the sound and not the letter name.* "Let's try one. What sound do you hear at the end of *mat*?" /t/ If the child provides an incorrect response, assist them by using the language in the first prompt. If the child provides the correct response, continue. "Now let's try some more." Read the below sets of words. Record the child's responses.		
	1. green	3. fall	
	2. foot	4. good	

	Sounds Part II
Segmenting	"I am going to tell you a word and you are going to break the sounds apart. If I say dog, I want you to say /d/ /o/ /g/." (You may use counting chips to demonstrate, allowing the child to touch or slide one for each sound they hear). Demonstrate for the child. "Let's try one. *Jam*. Can you pull the sounds apart?" /j/ /a/ /m/ If the child's response is incorrect, guide in understanding the task and provide the correct response. If correct, move on to attempt more words. "Now let's try a few more. I will tell you a word and you will break it apart to tell me each sound you hear." Continue with the word set below and record the child's responses. Remember e-gg and a-pe, have 2 sounds. {| 1. egg	3. ape |} {| 2. bat	4. pan |}
Blending	"Now I will tell you some sounds and you are going to put them together to make a word. If I say /r/ /a/ /t/ then you will say *rat*. "Let's try one. /f/ /a/ /n/. Can you put the sounds together?" *Fan* If the child's response is incorrect, guide in understanding the task and provide the correct response. If correct, move on to attempt more words. "Now let's try a few more. I will tell you some sounds and you will put them together to make a word." Continue with the word set below and record the child's responses. {| 1. /b/ /ee/	3. /v/ /a/ /n/ |} {| 2. /t/ /a/ /g/	4. /z/ /i/ /p/ |}

Student Name: _____	Date Assessed: _____		
\multicolumn{4}{c}{**Rhymes**}			

Recognition	jet - pet		car - cat		
	red - ran		bug - hug		/4
Production	bag		dad		
	rub		nut		/4
\multicolumn{6}{c}{**Sounds Part I**}					
Initial	hat - hill		money - map		
	dog - duck		look - line		/4
Final	green		good		
	foot		fall		/4
Subtotal					
\multicolumn{6}{c}{**Sounds Part II**}					
Segment	egg (e-gg)		ape (a-pe)		
	bat (b-a-g)		pan (p-a-n)		/4
Blend	/b/ /ee/ (bee)		/v/ /a/ /n/ (van)		
	/t/ /a/ /g/ (tag)		/z/ /i/ /p/ (zip)		/4
Subtotal					/8

Appendix B

Concepts of Print Assessment

Teacher Directions

> Materials:
> - Student assessment pages
> - Teacher recording tables
>
> Directions:
>
> **Letters vs. Words**
> 1. "I am going to ask you to point to some letters, words, shapes, and numbers for me."
> 2. Using student pages 1–2, ask:
>   "Can you point to just one letter for me?"
>   "Can you point to a picture for me?"
>   "Can you point to a word for me?"
>   "Can you point to a number for me?"
>   "Can you point to a sentence for me?"
> 3. Record their responses on the recording page.
> 4. Repeat with second student page.

Print vs. Pictures and Sentences
5. Say, "I am going to show you a page with a picture and writing, then I will ask you to show me how we can read it together."
6. "Can you point to the picture?"
7. "Where can I find the words?"
8. "If I want to read this with you, where should I begin? Can you point to where I should start reading?"
9. "Can you use your finger to show me which way (direction) I should go?"
10. "What happens when I get to the end of this first line?" (Point to the end of the line; the child should point to the start of the next line. If they provide a verbal prompt, ask them to point.)

Student Name: _____
Date Assessed: _____

Letters vs. Words (Use Student Page Letters vs Words- Child w/Backpack, "Blue, " K", "12)

"Can you point to just one letter for me?"	k	S	/2
"Can you point to a picture for me?"	child	bicycle	/2
"Can you point to a word for me?"	blue	hot	/2
"Can you point to a number for me?"	12	8	/2
"Can you point to a sentence for me?"	I want…	I like…	/2

Print vs. Pictures and Sentences (Use Student Page Print vs. Pictures- Picture of Apple + Sentence)

"Can you point to the picture?"	Points to the apples	/1
"Where can I find where the words are to read?"	Points under the words	/1
"If I want to read this with you, where should I begin? Can you point to where I should start reading?"	Points to start of the first sentence.	/1
"Can you use your finger to show me which way (direction) I should go?"	Swipes left to right.	/1
"What happens when I get to the end of this first line?" (Point to the end of the line.)	Points to the start of the next line.	/1

Appendix B ◆ 127

Student Page 1 Letters vs Words

blue

12

k

I want a red bicycle.

Student Page 2 Letters vs Words

| 8 | S |

| hot | 🚲 |

I like to build with blocks.

Student Page Print vs. Pictures

I love eating apples. They are sweet and red.

Appendix C

Materials:
- Student assessment pages
- Teacher recording tables

Directions:
1. Cover the sentence and say, "I am going to say a sentence, and I want you to say it after me. 'This is a chair.' Now you say it."
2.

CORRECT RESPONSE:	INCORRECT RESPONSE:
(This is a chair.)	Say, "Listen again as I say this sentence so that you can say it. 'This is a chair.'"
Say, "Very good."	If the correct response is not given, repeat.

3. Uncover the print and say, "The sentence below this picture [Point to the sentence] tells what is happening in the picture. Watch. I will read the sentence and use my special pointer to point to the words." (Use a popsicle stick to point to each word. Read the *first* sentence and point to each word.) "This is a chair."

    "Now, I will do it again, but this time I will ask you to do it just like me. Watch carefully." (Read the first sentence and point to each word.)

    "Now you do it. Say the sentence and point to each word. Start here." (Move the child's popsicle stick to the first word.)

CORRECT RESPONSE:	INCORRECT RESPONSE
(Child points to each word as he/she says it. Their finger can be placed anywhere on the word, not just the beginning.) "Very good. You pointed to each word!"	"Watch as I point to each word. This is a chair. Now you do it." If response is still incorrect then say, "Let's do it together. Follow my finger." (Put your finger above the words and ask the child to point and say the words as you say them.)

4. Ask the child, "Can you point to the word ___?" Record the child's responses.

5. Continue the same procedure for each of the sentences. Make sure that the child is watching when you fingerpoint. *You can repeat the reading and pointing if needed.* Assign one point for each word correctly pointed to.

Student Name:
Date Assessed:

Sentence	Finger Pointing[1]	Word Finding[2]
This is a chair.	sample	
These are grapes.	___/3	grapes ___/1
Pears are green.	___/3	green ___/1
Red apples are yummy.	___/4	___Red ___are ___/2
I like blueberries.	___/3	like ___/1
Bananas are sweet and yellow.	___/5	sweet ___yellow ___/2
Subtotals	___/18	___/7
Grand Total		/25

1 Assign 1 point for each word that the student correctly points to *while saying the word*.

2 Assign 1 point for each word that the student can relocate after "fingerpoint" reading the line.

Appendix C ◆ 133

This is a chair.

These are grapes.

Pears are green.

Red apples are yummy.

I like blueberries.

Bananas are sweet and yellow.

Appendix D

Letter Names

Student Name: _____
Date Assessed: _____

Materials:
- student assessment pages
- teacher recording tables

Directions:
1. Present the child with the Uppercase letter cards, presenting one set at a time.
2. Tell the child that you will point to a letter and you want them to tell you its **name**.
 *"I'm going to point to a letter and I want you to tell me it's **name**."*
 (Ex. /em/ for M)
1. Record their responses in the boxes to the right. If they say an incorrect response, record what they did say. For correct answers, place a checkmark in the box.

Children < 4 years: If the child misses more than 3 in a set, stop the assessment or present with the next cards, but prompt with "Do you recognize any of these letters? Can you tell me their name?
Children 4+: Attempt the whole assessment.

Repeat with lowercase letters.

Results
Letter Name Identification:
Uppercase: ____/26
Lowercase: ____/26

	Identification Uppercase
O	
B	
A	
X	
S	
R	
C	
M	
K	
E	
P	
D	
H	
T	
W	
L	
Z	
F	
Y	
J	
G	
N	
Q	
I	
U	
V	

	Identification Lowercase
o	
x	
c	
s	
k	
w	
z	
i	
e	
y	
m	
p	
r	
f	
v	
u	
j	
a	
n	
h	
t	
g	
b	
l	
d	
q	

Appendix D ◆ 141

Student Name: _____
Date Assessed: _____

Letter Sounds

Materials:
- student assessment pages
- teacher recording table

Directions:
Begin with Uppercase Letter Sounds. If child has accurately identified at least 15 letters, assess for sound identification.

1. Present the child with the Uppercase letter sound cards, presenting one set at a time.
2. Tell the child that you will point to a letter and you want them to tell **you what sound it makes.**

"Now I am going to point to a letter and I want you to tell me what *sound* that letter tells you to say." (Ex. /m/ for M)

1. Record their responses in the boxes to the right. If they say an incorrect response, record what they did say. For correct answers, place a checkmark in the box.

If child misses more than 3 in a set, stop and present the cards asking for them to point to ones they know rather than you pointing to each letter.

Repeat with lowercase the child accurately identified at least 15 lowercase letter names.

For the younger children, you may alternatively point to the letters they identified the letter names of (rather than all of them), asking them now to identify the sound.

Results:

Sound Identification:
Uppercase: ____/26
Lowercase: ____/26

	Sound Uppercase	
B		
T		
J		
K		
D		
A	long	short
E	long	short
I	long	short
O	long	short
U	long	short
P		
G	hard	soft
V		
Z		
C	hard	soft
L		
F		
M		
R		
S		
N		
H		
Y		
W		
X		
Q		

	Sound Lowercase	
b		
t		
j		
k		
d		
a	long	short
e	long	short
i	long	short
o	long	short
u	long	short
p		
g	hard	soft
v		
z		
c	hard	soft
l		
f		
m		
r		
s		
n		
h		
y		
w		
x		
q		

Uppercase Letter Name-Student Page

Appendix D ◆ 143

Lowercase Letter Name Student Page

144 ◆ Appendix D

Uppercase Letter Sound Name Student Page

Appendix D ◆ 145

Lowercase Letter Sound Identification-Student Page

| Bb | Tt | Jj | Kk | Dd |

| Aa | Ee | Ii | Oo | Uu |

| Pp | Gg | Vv | Zz | Cc |

| Ll | Ff | Mm | Rr | Ss |
| Nn |

| Hh | Yy | Ww | Xx | Qq |

Upper/Lower Letter Sound Identification-Student Page